TERRY OTTEN

THE CRIME OF INNOCENCE
IN THE FICTION
OF TONI MORRISON

A LITERARY FRONTIERS EDITION, NO. 33

UNIVERSITY OF MISSOURI PRESS

COLUMBIA AND LONDON

Library of Congress Cataloging-in-Publication Data

Otten, Terry.
      The crime of innocence in the fiction of Toni Morrison /
Terry Otten.
            p.   cm. — (A Literary frontiers edition ; no. 33)
            ISBN 0-8262-0711-1 (alk. paper)
            1. Morrison, Toni—Criticism and interpretation. I. Title.
II. Series.
PS3563.O8749Z8   1989
813'.54—dc20   89-4851
                                                                      CIP

ACKNOWLEDGMENTS

I am indebted to faculty and student colleagues for insights, sug-
gestions, and not a little patience; to the Thomas Library staff, and
especially Kathy Schulz and Velma Layman, for many a kind assist; to
Shirley Wilson for typing my manuscript in good order; to the Witten-
berg University Research Fund Board for financial assistance; and to
the Editor of *Studies in American Fiction* for permission to reprint portions of an essay on *Tar Baby* published in that journal. As always, I
owe most to Jane—for her good ear, right questions, and constant
encouragement.

The Bluest Eye by Toni Morrison. Copyright © 1970 by Toni Morrison.
Excerpts reprinted by permission of Holt, Rinehart and Winston, Inc.

Sula by Toni Morrison. Copyright © 1973 by Toni Morrison. Excerpts
reprinted by permission of Alfred A. Knopf, Inc.

Song of Solomon by Toni Morrison. Copyright © 1977 by Toni Morrison.
Excerpts reprinted by permission of Alfred A. Knopf, Inc.

Tar Baby by Toni Morrison. Copyright © 1981 by Toni Morrison.
Excerpts reprinted by permission of Alfred A. Knopf, Inc.

Beloved by Toni Morrison. Copyright © 1987 by Toni Morrison.
Excerpts reprinted by permission of Alfred A. Knopf, Inc.

FOR JANE, FOR KEITH AND KATE, FOR JULIE
—beloved all

CONTENTS

THE CRIME OF INNOCENCE

IN THE FICTION

OF TONI MORRISON

INTRODUCTION

ALTHOUGH she secured her place as an important black novelist with the publication of *Song of Solomon* in 1977, Toni Morrison has not always been accorded the respect most feel she merits. When she failed to win the National Book Award for *Beloved* in 1987, forty-nine black writers published a protest letter in a *New York Times* advertisement, implying that Morrison had been the victim of prejudice. For most critics, black and white, an injustice was done to a work that was later to win the Pulitzer Prize for Fiction. Those few critics who have not acknowledged Morrison's place as a major novelist have tended to level two charges against her fiction: that it is melodramatic and morally simplistic. Neither is the case.

Though denying a "monolithic prescription of what black literature is or ought to be," Morrison does seek to produce a literature "irrevocably, indisputably Black."[1] She complains about critics who compare her work to the accepted canon of modern literature, attempt to apply rigid critical theories to her work, or praise her according to "criteria from other paradigms" than those reflecting the black culture she represents.[2] "Critics of my work have often left something to be desired," she has said, "because they don't always evolve out of the culture, the world, the given quality out of which I write."[3] Yet Morrison equally condemns the potentially reductive tendencies of racially defined art. "Black writers always explained something to someone else," she has com-

1. Toni Morrison, "Memory, Creation, and Writing," *Thought*, December 1984, 359.
2. Toni Morrison, "Rootedness: The Ancestor as Foundation," in *Black Women Writers (1950–1980): A Critical Evaluation*, ed. Mari Evans (Garden City, N.Y.: Anchor Press/Doubleday, 1984), 342.
3. Nellie McKay, "An Interview with Toni Morrison," *Contemporary Literature* 24, no. 4 (1983): 425.

mented. "And I didn't want to explain anything to anybody else! I mean, if I could understand it, then I assumed two things: (a) that other Black people could understand it and (b) that White people, if I was any good, could understand it also."[4] Noting another pitfall of self-consciously ethnic literature, she has said, "I recognize and despise the artificial black writing some writers do. I feel them slumming among black people."[5]

For Morrison, the artistic struggle involves achieving the balance between writing a truly black literature and producing a fiction that, in Faulkner's phrase, "grieves on universal bones." As Cynthia Davis has concluded, Morrison's "fictions try to combine existential concerns compatible with a mythic presentation with an analysis of American society." In particular, she goes on to observe, "Morrison's allusions to traditional Western myth . . . correct it by showing how far the dominant culture has come from its roots, and emphasize the denial of responsibility in the faceless anti-myth."[6] According to Morrison herself:

> If my work is to confront a reality unlike that received reality of the West, it must centralize and animate information discredited by the West—discredited not because it is not true or useful or even of some racial value, but because it is information described as "lore" or "gossip" or "magic" or "sentiment."[7]

Morrison transforms societal myths of American materialistic culture with the earned wisdom of a people grown wise through suffering. At once polemical and mythic, her novels juxtapose unrelenting realism and the

4. Jane Bakerman, "The Seams Can't Show: An Interview with Toni Morrison," *Black American Literature Forum* 12 (1978): 39.

5. Claudia Tate, "Toni Morrison," in *Black Women Writers*, ed. Claudia Tate (New York: Continuum, 1983), 118.

6. "Self, Society, and Myth in Toni Morrison's Fiction," *Contemporary Literature* 23, no. 3 (1982): 334–35.

7. "Memory, Creation, and Writing," 388.

transcendent authority of mythic truth. A source of the mythic substructure of her fiction is most certainly the Bible, if not the conventional interpretation of its meaning. Acknowledging her upbringing in a highly religious family whose "resources were biblical," Morrison has noted that her family combined the Bible with other sources. "They did not limit themselves to understanding the word only through Christian theology."[8] Her novels similarly reflect an amalgamation of mythic matter, depicting a world couched at times in seemingly contradictory truths: rebels becoming heroes, good creating evil; gardens that oppress, sins that redeem. They preserve the essential truth of myth by ironically modifying or reversing more orthodox assumptions of meaning.

Morrison has remarked, "I like to work with, to fret, the cliché because the experience expressed in it is important. . . . Most of the books that are about something—the books that mean something—treat old ideas, old situations."[9] The oldest of ideas may be the parable of the fall and its related themes: the quest for identity, initiation and the passage from innocence to experience, the nature of good and evil, the ambiguity of the garden and the serpent, the paradoxical consequences of self-knowledge. Indeed, these integrating themes encompass all of Morrison's fiction, as she adapts the elements of the fall paradigm to describe the emerging selfhood in black characters trapped in a white society, often fusing these timeless motifs with African myth and fantasy. To survive, her protagonists must somehow violate the rule of the oppressive system, reject the values it venerates, and recover the human potential denied to blacks.

Though by no means imitating the romantic poets, Morrison creates a parallel view of a fortunate fall: the necessary and potentially redemptive passage from a gar-

8. Bessie W. Jones, "An Interview with Toni Morrison," in Bessie W. Jones and Audrey L. Vinson, *The World of Toni Morrison* (Dubuque, Iowa: Kendall/Hunt, 1985), 137.
9. Thomas LeClair, "'The Language Must Not Sweat,'" *The New Republic*, 21 March 1981, 26.

den state of debilitating innocence to painful self-knowledge and its consequences. But whereas romantic writers tended to see the fall more essentially as personal experience than the embodiment of communal myth, Morrison sees the fortunate fall as a return to the true community or "village" consciousness. The victorious end for her involves not only the escape from the white man's Eden but the discovery of the black consciousness muted in a white society. Certainly Morrison understands well what the romantics learned long ago, that in a society operated by an oppressive order, not to sin in the conventional sense perpetuates an immoral justice. In such a world innocence is itself a sign of guilt, because it signals a degenerate acquiescence. Not to fall becomes more destructive than to fall. Those of her characters who accept the debunked values of the dominant white culture construct or escape to spurious Edens: the quintessential white middle-class "Dick-and-Jane" house, as well as Geraldine's imitation of it, and the pretentious Fisher estate where Pauline Breedlove evades her blackness in *The Bluest Eye*; the proper if sterile Wright house in *Sula*; the Deads' house and the "nigger heaven" Honoré Island in *Song of Solomon*; the white man's paradise Isle de Chevalier in *Tar Baby*; the deceptive Sweet Home in *Beloved*.

And those who disrupt these Edenic worlds play the ambiguous role of serpent in a specious paradise. Morrison's novels often present us with conventionally evil characters, outsiders in a decadent, white-dominated culture, Cains and Liliths in the guise of Cholly Breedlove or Sula Peace or Guitar Bains or Son Green or Sethe Suggs. On the one hand, characters of potential violence or cruelty and, on the other hand, rebels against a morally deficient system, each one tells us in unequivocal terms that evil can be redemptive and that goodness can be enslaving. In the language of existential theology, those who sin against the flawed order become the agents of experience and so run the risk of freedom. Those who do not are often doomed to spiritual stasis and moral en-

4

tropy. For Morrison herself has stated, "Evil is as useful as good" and "Sometimes good looks like evil; and sometimes evil looks like good."[10]

Although she unreservedly indicts materialistic white culture and severely judges those blacks who adopt its values, Morrison's fictions are not simplistic polemics on the viciousness generated by white society. Morrison's work exceeds mere invective. At their most profound level, the novels penetrate the characters themselves, exposing their capacity for cowardice and corruption. Rather than remaining sympathetic victims, her characters generally become responsible for their actions—or inactions. In all her novels the fall from innocence becomes a necessary gesture of freedom and a profound act of self-awareness. It assumes the nature of a potentially tragic action, a paradoxical victory and defeat. It is perhaps significant that Morrison, a classics major in college, labels her works "tragic," for her characters confront tragic choice, in which any decision entails a loss. Driven by the imperative to honor the demands of a moral absolutism and by the counter impulse to act on behalf of self, her protagonists either suffer the consequences of innocence, as Nel Wright does, or run the risk of freedom, as Milkman Dead. The tragic drama of a fortunate fall is played out in a setting conditioned by the tyrannical morality and values of its white god. In short, each novel describes a fall wrought with destruction but one that is still morally superior to prolonged self-ignorance and sterile accommodation.

Of course, the theme of the fall has been part of American literature from its beginnings. As critics have long noted, humanity's depraved condition has been an essential concern of writers from Edwards to Hawthorne, Poe, James, O'Neill, and Dickey. Studies such as Robert Spiller's *The Cycle of American Literature* (1955), R. W. B.

10. Robert B. Stepto, "'Intimate Things in Place': A Conversation with Toni Morrison," in *Chant of Saints: A Gathering of Afro-American Literature, Art, and Scholarship*, ed. Michael S. Harper and Robert B. Stepto (Urbana: University of Illinois Press, 1979), 216.

5

Lewis's *The American Adam* (1955), Sacvan Bercovitch's *The Puritan Origins of the American Self* (1975) and *The American Jeremiad* (1981), and William Shurr's *Rappaccini's Daughter* (1981) have explored the persistence and variation of the fall and related themes in recent as well as earlier American literature. While Morrison shares an affinity with Romantic writers, she is of course directly influenced by the rich oral resources of Afro-American myth and the writings of black authors, especially female writers like Frances Harper and Zora Neale Hurston, who strongly portray the dilemma of growing up black and female in America. In adapting and modifying the traditional fall pattern to fit her conception of the black experience in contemporary American society, Morrison does not restrict so much as enlarge her vision, incorporating the peculiar features of the black experience in a universal mythic perspective. In particular, Morrison projects a fortunate fall idea through characters who must destroy the false identity ascribed them as blacks in a spurious "garden." Those co-opted by the system, such as Pauline Breedlove or Helene Wright or Macon Dead, or those totally victimized by it, such as Pecola Breedlove, suffer unredeemable defeat. Only those courageous enough and strong enough to risk freedom gain a measure of victory.

While by no means intending to reduce the rich complexity and dense texture of the works, my purpose here is to trace the evolution and variety of the fall pattern in Morrison's novels and to examine it as an encompassing myth incorporating other major themes and motifs. The novels do not follow a simple paradigmatic structure or emphasize equally the given characteristics of the fall pattern. Nor does the idea of a fall fully or adequately describe the achievement of Morrison's art. Nonetheless, all the works portray basic features of the fall. They contain gardens emblematic of a state of innocence, serpent figures projecting the unconscious self, duality portraying the paradoxical nature of good and evil, the nakedness of conscious awareness, and the ambiguity of existence east of Eden. Morrison's use of the myth to depict the plight and possible transcendence of her black protagonists in American society imbues her fiction with realism and universality.

THE BLUEST EYE

THE Bluest Eye first introduces Morrison's concern with what she calls in *Tar Baby* "the crime of innocence."[1] In her sensitive portrayal of the perilous transition from innocence to experience, she provides a penetrating insight into the essential integrating theme in her fiction, the paradox of good and evil—the potential of innocence to incapacitate and the power of "evil" to free the self. In the subsequent novels conventionally "good" characters are sometimes empowered to act by conventionally "evil" ones. Sula, Guitar, Son, and Beloved become poles in the dialectic, galvanizing their Others into action. While threatening their counterparts by their own will to power, they nonetheless make self-discovery possible. In effect, the later novels fully examine the implication of lost innocence that *The Bluest Eye* first introduces in its characterization of failed initiation.

The headnote frames the work in caricature. In mock primer style it describes the idyllic middle-class American family. Mother, Father, Dick, and Jane live in material comfort in a green-and-white house complete with cat and dog. A friend comes to play with Jane, the child Pecola Breedlove yearns to be. Ironically foreshadowing the annihilation of Pecola's doomed dream to enter this paradise, the primer collapses into unpunctuated sentences and finally dissolves into a jumble of unspaced letters. The fractured language anticipates Pecola's cruel experience at the Fisher house, where she is first rejected by the light-skinned Fisher girl—a reflection of Shirley Temple and the yellow-haired, Mary-Jane-candy model whom Pecola wants to resemble—then more traumatically by her own mother. It forecasts as well the humiliating defeat she endures as a "nasty little black bitch" when she

1. *Tar Baby* (New York: Alfred A. Knopf, 1981), 242.

unwittingly ventures into the proper Geraldine's imitation Dick-and-Jane house. Ostracized from the American dream by virtue of her blackness and from a black community too much corrupted by the values of the white culture, she can only succeed in her insanity, having borne the effects of a devastating fall. Her violent passage from innocence to experience ironically results in the perpetual innocence of insanity that alone can grant her the "blue eyes" which will assure her acceptance.

Morrison presents the theme of failed innocence in the opening words of the narrative. Claudia, the principal narrator, summarizes the consequences of the tale she is about to tell, the story of Cholly Breedlove's incestuous rape of his daughter, Pecola (the close friend of Claudia and her sister Frieda), of the death of Pecola's illicit baby, of Cholly's death and Pecola's eventual madness: "Cholly Breedlove is dead; our innocence too."[2] The narrative recounts not only the painful initiation of the three girls, but includes stories of other falls as well, of the lost innocence of Cholly Breedlove and his wife, Pauline, of the respectable "colored" Geraldine, and of Soaphead Church. As is typical in Morrison's works, *The Bluest Eye* intersperses biographical sketches of individual characters throughout the narrative, amplifying themes and providing counterpoint to the central plot.

As Claudia recounts the events of 1940–1941, when she was nine years old, Frieda ten, and Pecola eleven, she offers the ingenuous viewpoint of a black girl growing up in a small town of the northern Midwest. Morrison weaves the chronology of seasons from autumn to autumn into Claudia's narration to underline its mythic pattern, the stages of initiation from childhood innocence to experience. Even Claudia's brief prefatory comment that begins, "Quiet as it's kept, there were no marigolds in the fall of 1941" (3), signals for us the consequences of an unredeemed fall, the dry infertility that comes regardless

2. *The Bluest Eye* (New York: Holt, Rinehart and Winston, 1970), 3. Page numbers hereafter in parentheses in the text.

of the ritual sacrifice of Pecola's baby. And Claudia's account ironically reverses the seasonal sequence of the tragic pattern, for in the fall of 1941 Claudia had undergone a rite of passage, discovering the harsh reality that her and Frieda's "innocence and faith" could not save Pecola's child or guarantee that the marigolds would blossom "and everything would be all right." Neither the seeds she and Frieda planted in the spring nor the seed Cholly planted "in his plot of black dirt" could assure life. The fall brings death, not harvest.

In the "Autumn" section of the story, set in 1940, Pecola and the MacTeer girls undergo a series of initiations that point toward Pecola's fateful encounter with her father the following spring. Not the least of these is Pecola's first "ministration," which prepares her to receive her father's seed. Set in a context when Claudia already is considering "the number of boyfriends" she will have and when the girls contemplate going to look at Mr. Henry's "girlie magazines" in the room he rents from the MacTeers, the event symbolizes the girls' passage from childhood. Having been told by Frieda that she can now have a baby but "somebody has to love you," Pecola wonders "how do you get somebody to love you?" (23). The question foreshadows Cholly's rape of his daughter; even here, Morrison suggests that the violation to come is itself paradoxical, that it is an act of love as well as brutality.

The "Autumn" section includes other initiations as well. One event in particular describes Pecola's discovery that her blackness excludes her from the love and acceptance she seeks in the society caricatured by the primer. Having already been made to feel like an ugly pariah, despised at school, rejected by her parents, she prays for the Shirley Temple storybook-blue eyes that would transform her ugliness and earn her parents' love. One day she goes down Garden Avenue to buy Mary Jane candies from Mr. Yacobowski. The street is symbolically named; for Pecola it is indeed a garden "buffeted by the familiar and therefore loved images" (35). The dandelions, the Y-crack in the sidewalk, the "other intimate things" she sees and experiences on Garden Avenue give reassurance. She owns the crack in the sidewalk and the clumps of dandelions that others think ugly, "and owning them made her part of the world, and the world a part of her" (36). But her paradise collapses under the weight of knowledge. When she tries to buy the Mary Jane candies with the blond-haired, white-faced, blue-eyed girl looking "out of a world of clean comfort" (38), she confronts Mr. Yacobowski's smeary blue eyes, which despise her for her blackness. Leaving the store with knowledge of her ugly blackness, she feels "inexplicable shame." She finds Garden Avenue a shattered paradise. The dandelions with which she identifies herself suddenly "*are* ugly." "They *are* weeds" (37), she now realizes, as she trips over the once comforting crack in the sidewalk. To resist the shame she feels, a crimeless guilt, she eats the candy to acquire Mary Jane's eyes, to *be* Mary Jane.

Significantly, Morrison ends the first section with Pecola's visit to the three whores who live above the Breedloves: the "merry gargoyles" Maginot Line (Marie), Poland, and China. These "merry harridans" directly contrast with their polar opposites, the self-righteous respectable women represented by the "colored" Geraldine. Despite their coarseness, they welcome Pecola, whereas Geraldine casts Pecola out of her protected garden. Lacking the hypocrisy of women who "deceive their husbands" or deny their own sexual desires, the three are "amused by a long ago time of innocence"—they have "no word for innocence" (42–43). Marie tells Pecola stories "because she was a child"; but when Pecola asks if she and her "fabled" lover, Dewey Prince, had children, Marie exposes her own lost innocence. She fidgets and begins to pick her teeth, which "meant she didn't want to talk anymore" (43). Toughened by experience, the whores live beyond innocence; but they cannot protect Pecola from brutalizing self-awareness. They offer a measure of knowledge, but not redemption. When Pecola looks out their window onto a world rapidly turning to winter, she sees that a "tuft of grass had forced its way up through a crack in the sidewalk, only to meet a raw October wind" (43–44). Emblematic of Pecola's rapidly fading childhood, the world moves toward death as Pecola inches toward a fall.

Two major events in the "Winter" portion of the novel point directly to Cholly's rape of Pecola, and in both Morrison depicts how American society has substituted beauty for virtue, describing how even the black community has allowed itself to be corrupted by a simplistic notion that devalues human beings solely on condition of their seeming ugliness. In such a perverse value system, blackness is aligned with ugliness, and expunging it becomes a basis for acceptability. "The concept of physical beauty as a virtue is one of the dumbest, most pernicious and destructive ideas of the Western world," Morrison has commented. "The point about concentrating on whether we are beautiful is that it is a concentration on a way of measuring worth that is wholly trivial and wholly white."[3] On the verge of self-awareness, Pecola is dangerously naive and fully capable of accepting the idea that a socially defined beauty alone merits love. Her childish belief compels her to become a blue-eyed Shirley Temple to secure beauty and counterbalance the blackness that makes her ugly. Morrison has said that Pecola "wanted to do that white trip because of the society in which she lived and, very importantly, because of the black people who helped her want to be that."[4] In her childish if largely accurate view, Pecola understands that blackness excludes

3. "Behind the Making of *The Black Book*," *Black World*, February 1974, 89. Barbara Christian remarks that "by exploring the devastating effects the Western ideas of beauty and romantic love have on a vulnerable black girl," Morrison "demonstrates how those ideas can invert the moral order of an entire culture. . . . Pecola becomes the scapegoat for that part of us that needs to see our fears of unworthiness embodied in some form" (*Black Women Novelists: The Development of a Tradition, 1892–1976* [Westport, Conn.: Greenwood Press, 1980], 152–53).

4. Robert B. Stepto, "'Intimate Things in Place': A Conversation with Toni Morrison," in *Chant of Saints: A Gathering of Afro-American Literature, Art, and Scholarship*, ed. Michael S. Harper and Robert B. Stepto (Urbana: University of Illinois Press, 1979), 223.

12

her from the American Eden. Her encounters with Maureen Peal and Geraldine demonstrate how blacks have been victimized by what Blake called "mind forg'd manacles."

Maureen Peal embodies the inverted values of the dominant American culture, so it is no wonder that Claudia as narrator associates her with a false spring rather than the winter or death she truly represents. Claudia recalls that while she and Frieda "waited for Spring, when there could be gardens," the arrival of the "high-yellow dream child," Maureen, disrupts the seasons. Identified with the successful white culture (she "even bought and liked white milk"), she is rich by black standards, "swaddled in comfort and care." The other blacks "adore" and envy Maureen because she possesses the beauty and wealth that define success. They reject Pecola Breedlove because she possesses neither. One "false spring day, which, like Maureen, had pierced the shell of deadening winter," Claudia, Frieda, and Maureen witness a group of boys harassing Pecola. In "their contempt for their own blackness," the boys make Pecola the scapegoat "of their smoothly cultivated ignorance, their exquisitely learned self-hatred, their elaborately designed hopelessness" (50). When they see Maureen's "springtime eyes," they stop tormenting Pecola, though it is Frieda and Claudia who come to their friend's defense. The boys' feeble retreat pays homage to Maureen's portrayal of the American dream.

Not insignificantly, Maureen tells the three girls about "Pecola" in the movie *Imitation of Life*, but unlike the young, very black girl, the "imitation" Pecola "was so pretty." When the girls pass a poster of Betty Grable at the Dreamland Theater, Maureen asks, "Don't you just love her?" (53). Like Pecola's mother, Pauline, Maureen Peal buys into the dream world of the American culture, which excludes the three truly black girls. When Maureen buys Pecola an ice cream cone to find out if she really did see her father naked, as the taunting boys had claimed, Pecola "seemed to fold into herself, like a pleated wing"

(57), once again expelled from paradise. Even Claudia and Frieda, who defend Pecola against Maureen's accusation that she saw "her old black daddy" naked, cannot escape the emerging truth that in this society they are pariahs. They "were sinking under the wisdom, accuracy, and relevance" of Maureen's last words: "I *am* cute! And you ugly! Black and ugly black e mos" (56). They move to the very end of childlike innocence, aware that though they might in rage destroy the white dolls given them by black parents at Christmas and might struggle to believe in their own worth, they cannot deny the reality that in the inverted world black is ugly. As Claudia recalls, they barely cling to a fading innocence:

> Dolls we could destroy, but we could not destroy the honey voices of parents and aunts, the obedience in the eyes of our peers, the slippery light in the eyes of our teachers when they encountered the Maureen Peals of the world. . . . Guileless and without vanity, we were still in love with ourselves then. We felt comfortable in our skins, enjoyed our dirt, cultivated our scars, and could not comprehend our unworthiness. . . . And all the time we knew that Maureen Peal was not the Enemy and was not worthy of such intense hatred. The *Thing* to fear was the *Thing* that made *her* beautiful, and not us. (57–58)

The perversity that conceals itself as "a false spring day" in Maureen Peal finds full expression in Geraldine. To preserve her innocence, Geraldine "will build her nest stick by stick, make it her own inviolable world, and stand guard over its every plant, weed, and doily" (65). She is one of those prim and proper "colored" women who come from Mobile, or Meridian, or Aiken who do not "sweat in [their] armpits nor between [their] thighs"; who do not "drink, smoke and swear"; who go to land-grant colleges to "learn to do the white man's work with refinement"; and who meticulously develop "thrift, patience, high morals, and good manners" to guard against "the dreadful funkiness of passion, the funkiness of na-

14

ture, the funkiness of the wide range of human emotions" (64). Married to a responsible and safe man, Geraldine represents the sexless, pure, acceptable "colored" women who deny their blackness in order to maintain their place in society. Like other such women, she owns a cat, a parody of the Dick-and-Jane pet, who responds to her love of "order, precision, and constancy." A substitute lover whose body warmth Geraldine lets "seep over and into the deeply private areas of her lap" (66), the cat symbolizes Geraldine's control, its blue eyes reflecting the whiteness Geraldine herself seeks. Her sole, obligatory son, the masochistic Junior, whom she forbids to play with "niggers," longs to smell "wild blackness" and to hear black boys say "'Fuck you' with that lovely casualness" (68), but he is powerless against his hated mother.

When Pecola wanders into Geraldine's tightly structured garden, she finds herself a stranger in paradise. Enticed by Junior to see some kittens, she enters an enchanted realm: one room is decorated with "a big red-and-gold Bible," lace doilies, potted plants, and a picture of Jesus Christ "hung on a wall with the prettiest pretend paper flowers fastened on the frame"; another room contains "a big lamp with green-and-gold base and white shades" and a rug on the floor with "enormous dark-red flowers" (69–70). Morrison makes clear that the house parodies the Dick-and-Jane house in the primer by fragmenting part of the primer passage as headnote to the scene.

With sudden maliciousness, Junior throws his mother's panicked cat into Pecola's face. After she extricates herself from its fierce claws, Pecola feels the cat, with its significantly blue eyes, rubbing against her leg. When she begins rubbing the cat in response to its affection, Junior quickly grabs the animal and, twirling it around, smashes it against the window and onto the radiator. When Geraldine suddenly returns, her son tells her that Pecola has killed the cat. Geraldine sees in Pecola the other self she has so long fought, the black self she so fears to be. Expelling Pecola from her sterile garden to maintain her own innocence, Geraldine calls the intruder a "nasty little

15

black bitch." In unmerited shame, Pecola backs out of the house and ironically sees "Jesus looking down at her with sad and unsurprised eyes" (72). The cat, Pecola, and Christ share a common fate, as Chikwenye Okonjo Ogunyemi has observed: "They know. The blue eyes of the black cat had not held Pecola for nothing—the cat and Pecola belong together in their helplessness and the experience of violence and injustice."[5] With Christ they suffer at the hands of righteousness. Although holding her head down against the cold March wind, Pecola cannot hold it low enough to avoid seeing the snowflakes "falling and dying on the pavement" (72). Like the "falling" and "dying" flakes that characterize her fallen state, she is prey to a world of violent rejection, her innocence shattered by growing awareness.

The "Autumn" and "Winter" portions of the novel tell of Claudia, Frieda, and Pecola's gradual passage from childlike innocence. Pecola's "ministration," her humiliation at Mr. Yacobowski's store, Maureen Peal's rejection of the girls, and Geraldine's condemnation of Pecola constitute painful rites of passage. All lead up to the rape, which Morrison places in the "Spring." The sacrificial death of Pecola's innocence in the planting of Cholly's seed produces melodrama, however, not high tragedy. For, unable to recover from her father's ambivalent act, Pecola retreats to the illusory Dick-and-Jane world.

Framing the violation, Morrison provides lengthy biographical sketches of the Breedloves that recount their own failed initiations and explain the inevitability of the event. Like many of Morrison's paired characters, the Breedloves provide mirror images of each other, parallel reflections against which they see themselves. Seeming opposites, they expose a duality that marks them as characters living after the fall. Their relationship impinges on each character's need—but inability—to embrace that part of the self the other represents. The tension between con-

5. "Order and Disorder in Toni Morrison's *The Bluest Eye*," *Critique* 19, no. 2 (1977): 116–17.

traries—good and evil, order and chaos, violence and passivity—characterize those who live beyond innocence. And the history of Cholly and Pauline explains the destructive power each brings to the relationship in consequence of that loss.

In a sense Cholly's innocence had never really existed. His father ran away before he was born, and his mother abandoned him on a junk heap. Raised by his Great Aunt Jimmy, Cholly was already cast from the garden. Thoroughly dependent on the kindness of his aunt and the gentle old Blue Jack, who worked with him at the grain store, he never really belonged. He especially felt ostracized from the dominant white society and its judgmental god. As a boy he felt nothing "thinking about God," but "just the idea of the devil excited him" (105). He was thrilled by the looming figure of a tall black father about to shatter a watermelon by throwing it down on stones, "blotting out the sun and getting ready to split open the world" (105). Nor could his tenuous innocence long endure in a culture conditioned by brutishness and oppression. In a carefully structured scene, Morrison describes Cholly's inevitable passage from innocence to experience.

When Aunt Jimmy died, signaling the end of his childhood, Cholly went to the funeral, where he had his first sexual encounter, with his cousin Darlene. As she does in other scenes depicting violation, such as the scene at Mr. Yacobowski's store, Morrison creates an ironic setting of idyllic beauty and seeming peace. Darlene and Cholly ran joyfully across an open field and riverbed "lined with green" to reach a vineyard where Muscadine grew wildly. They "sank down in the green-and-purple grass on the edge of the pine woods" (114). While making love, they were suddenly discovered by white hunters who shone flashlights on them and forced Cholly to "get on wid it. An' make it good nigger, make it good" (116). Cholly's innocent lovemaking was transfigured into shame and guilt, not guilt caused by the sexual act, of course, but by his inability to act against the humiliation. Unable to fight the white hunters, he directed his hatred toward the one who "bore witness to his failure" (118). No longer innocent because he had gained the knowledge of his own powerlessness, he suffered shame in consequence of his fall. To recover his lost innocence, "he cultivated his hatred of Darlene" (118), who had convicted him of his fault.

Later Cholly undertook a mythical journey to find his lost father, a further testimony of his estrangement. Banished from his thinly guarded Eden, he sought his father "with no more thought than a chick leaving its shell" (119). After locating him in a Macon alley, though, Cholly merely found his expulsion confirmed when his father ignored him in favor of playing craps. Ironically, banishment itself was a form of freedom. No longer restrained by any laws of accommodation, Cholly "was truly free." He achieved what Morrison has called a "godlike state" beyond good and evil: "Cholly was free. Dangerously free. Free to feel whatever he felt—fear, guilt, shame, love, grief, pity. Free to be tender or violent, to whistle or weep" (125). At fourteen he was indeed free to choose, but such freedom carries with it the consequences of choice and, finally, self-judgment.

Soon after gaining his "dangerous freedom," Cholly met Pauline Williams, whose story describes another loss of innocence. Reared as one of eleven children, Pauline moved with her family from Alabama to Kentucky near the beginning of World War I. The oldest remaining girl at home, she happily dropped out of school to take care of the house and the twins Chicken and Pie. But her contented life faded shortly after the war when the twins went off to school. Adolescence came upon her, and she fantasized about a Presence who would someday "lead her away to the sea, to the city, to the woods . . . forever" (88). The Presence was to become Cholly, who came whistling by one day when she was leaning against the fence. He instinctively bent down to tickle her foot, which had been deformed after a rusty nail was punched through it when she was only two. After a time they married and moved to Lorain, Ohio, where the novel is set. But tension soon developed. Yearning for her past home, Pauline felt alienated and trapped in two rooms so small they could not be cared for inside a house without a yard. Cholly began to resent her dependence on him and began to drink. When she became pregnant with Sammy, Cholly temporarily softened in his treatment of her, but for Pauline "the loneliness of these two rooms had not gone away" (94). She sought escape at the movies and tried to imitate white movie stars, her mimicry foreshadowing Pecola's yearning to be like Shirley Temple and Maureen Peals' admiration of Betty Grable and "Pecola" in *Imitation of Life*. One day when Pauline had made herself up like Jean Harlow, a tooth suddenly dropped out. "Everything went then," she later recalled, and despairingly, she "settled down to just being ugly." She soon became pregnant with Pecola, whose appearance at birth projected Pauline's self-contempt. She simply remarked, *"Lord she was ugly"* (98). Separated from her happy past and convicted of an ugliness represented by her blackness, Pauline adopted a moral absolutism, holding tenaciously to her innocence and martyrdom to avoid self-judgment. She joined the ranks of other women in Morrison's fiction, the Geraldines and Helene Wrights, who confuse innocence with morality and virtue with self-repression.

By the time the novel begins, when Pecola is eleven, Pauline has already constructed her defense against her own shame. "Holding Cholly as a model of sin and failure, she bore him like a crown of thorns and her children like a cross" (98). She enhances her self-worth by working for the Fisher family, caring for their "pink and white" daughter and tending to their spurious garden home of "beauty, order, cleanliness, and praise." "Pauline's diligence on behalf of the white family was her obedience to God," Audrey Vinson accurately concludes, and "She saw her own family as an abstraction to her order, including her Christian rectitude."[6] Claudia recalls Pauline's

6. "Vacant Places: Setting in the Novels of Toni Morrison," in Bessie W. Jones and Audrey L. Vinson, *The World of Toni Morrison* (Dubuque, Iowa: Kendall/Hunt, 1985), 38.

transfigured blackness in the Fisher kitchen: "Mrs. Breedlove's skin showed like taffeta in the reflection of white porcelain, white woodwork, polished cabinets, and brilliant copperware" (83). Guardian of her adopted paradise, Polly, as she was called demeaningly by the Fishers, expresses outrage when Pecola spills a berry cobbler. Ignoring the burns on her daughter's legs, she knocks her to the floor and comforts the crying Fisher girl. Fittingly, the sundown is "spilling on the lake" (85) when Pecola stands outside the door barring her way to the white home where her mother chooses to live in servitude.

Through the criminality of her innocence, Pauline holds firmly to her uprightness. Because Cholly's weakness and drunkenness have become the measure of her righteousness, she "would never have forgiven Jesus" had Cholly stopped drinking. "She [needs] Cholly's sins desperately" (31). Yet, paradoxically, Pauline remains a divided self. She wants Cholly's touch in bed, though she will not admit it. And she knows that in their unrestrained lovemaking, *I be strong, I be pretty, I be young* (101). Her orgasms return her to a lost innocence, to childhood rich with the colors of life and celebration: berry stains on her dress, lemonade made with golden seeds, and streaks of green made by June bugs. But such rainbows of being are obscured by a specious self-righteousness that makes morality severe self-denial. It converts her love for Cholly into hate.

Cholly, of course, needs to hate her as well, so "he [can] leave himself in tack" (31). The "constantness, varietylessness, the sheer weight of sameness" (126) that Pauline venerates in defense of her morality drive him to remorse. So it is that their fights have become ceremonies wrought with a "darkly brutal formalism" in which "There [is] only the muted sound of falling things, and flesh on unsurprised flesh" (32). In this grotesque relationship the "sin" of the Other becomes a stay against chaos. And it is against this history of depravity and perversion that Pecola's violation occurs. It gives witness to a world already fallen.

20

On the fated day Cholly comes home drunk and sees Pecola washing dishes at the sink, scratching the back of her calf with her toe. He relives that moment of innocent love when he first saw Pauline leaning against the fence, instinctively tickled her deformed foot and kissed her leg. A surrogate lover, Pecola reawakens the "joy" and the "curiosity" he felt then. So Cholly "wanted to fuck her— tenderly. But the tenderness would not hold" (128). Writes Morrison, "the love of a free man is never safe"; existing in the contraries of good and evil, love and lust, Cholly could only fill "the matrix of her agony with death" (163). A profound expression of love, the rape is also an exercise of power and freedom, a protest against an unjust and repressive culture. Morrison has argued that in writing *The Bluest Eye* she tells us at the very beginning what happened because she wants us to see what the event means in the telling, "so when you get to the scene . . . it's almost irrelevant because I want you to look at him and see his love for his daughter and his powerlessness to help her pain. By that time his embrace, the rape, is all the gift he has left."[7] Only in Sethe's killing of Beloved does Morrison more poignantly delineate the paradoxical nature of good and evil.

Wanting to show "a little girl as a total and complete victim of whatever was around her,"[8] Morrison ends the tale of initiation with Pecola's final victimization at the hands of Soaphead Church, the former Elihue Micah Whitcomb now turned spiritualist. After her violation Pecola, in her madness, goes to him to ask for the blue eyes that represent harmony, joy, and beauty, eyes that signal worthiness and belonging. Pecola seeks self-respect and beauty to combat the "ugliness" identified with

7. Claudia Tate, "Toni Morrison," in *Black Women Writers*, ed. Claudia Tate (New York: Continuum, 1983), 125. In another interview Morrison has said, "I want, here, to talk about how painful it is and what the painful consequences are of distortion of love that isn't fructified, is held in, not expressed" (Jane Bakerman, "The Seams Can't Show: An Interview with Toni Morrison," *Black American Literature Forum* 12 [1978]: 60.).

8. Stepto, "'Intimate Things in Place,'" 219.

her blackness. Soaphead's own experiences allow him to understand and accept Pecola but to feel anger, too, at his impotence. A West Indian brought up by black Anglophiles who did all they could to deny their own blackness, priding themselves on the white strain in their line, Soaphead suffers deep psychological scars. When his young wife left him soon after their marriage, he eventually settled in Lorain where the women of the town considered his celibacy supernatural rather than unnatural. He liked to fondle little girls, but the gesture was "anything but lewd," and "his patronage of little girls smacked of innocence" (132). The once miscast Anglican priest now interprets dreams and doles out happiness as "a true Spiritualist and Psychic Reader, born with power" (137).

When Soaphead deceives Pecola into killing his landlord's mangy dog, another parody of the Dick-and-Jane tableau, Pecola takes it for a sign, leaving with the spiritualist's blessing. With penetrating insight, the shabby prophet writes to his god, protesting an "imperfect world" in which "Evil [exists] because God had created it" (137). The opposite of the black Devil/God that thrilled Cholly Breedlove in the image of a looming black father about to splatter a watermelon, Soaphead's Victorian god embodies all the pious propriety that Pauline worships as a defense against her blackness. Accusing his white god of not letting the little children come to him, Soaphead writes, "You forget now and then to be God." Because God denied Pecola her blue eyes, Soaphead vows to give them to her—"No one else will see her blue eyes. But *she* will" (144). Too weak to defeat the Victorian colonialism of his past, with its deprecation of anything black, Soaphead Church, as Morrison has remarked, believes "that if black people were more like white people they would be better off." He therefore grants Pecola her wish as "a kind of English, colonial, Victorian thing drilled into his head which he could not escape."[9]

Soaphead's letter brings much of the novel into focus.

9. Ibid., 223.

He writes to an assuredly white god who has indeed created an "imperfect world" where black children are convicted of ugliness solely by virtue of their being black. For a while Claudia and Frieda act in their rapidly fading innocence to save Pecola's unborn child. In contrast to all the adults, Claudia "felt a need for someone to want the black baby to live—just to counteract the universal love of white baby dolls, Shirley Temples, and Maureen Peals. And Frieda must have felt the same thing" (149). Ironically, the adult black community wills the death, responding to the same false value system that makes them give Shirley Temple dolls to their children and adore Maureen Peal. The rape creates a potentially "ugly" black baby, the love of which might have proved redemptive to Claudia and Frieda, who want the baby to live not despite but because of its blackness. Having moved through experience, they choose to accept Pecola's child, a child of "sin," but potentially a child of grace. But their naive efforts to bribe the silent god by being "good for a whole month" prove futile.

Claudia, now older, looks back knowing that, though brutally defeated, Pecola was the necessary surrogate that allowed others to exist. "We were so beautiful when we stood astride her ugliness," she recalls. "Even her waking dreams we used—to silence our nightmares. And she let us, and thereby deserved the contempt" (163). Morrison depicts Pecola more as victim than as genuinely tragic figure. Unable to commit a saving sin or protect herself against the prolonged self-hate of Cholly or Pauline or Geraldine, she falls prey to an evil beyond herself. Yet our compassion for her coexists with our awareness of her weakness. In the later novels Morrison presents older characters who must assume more responsibility for their destinies, though they too suffer in a degenerate world. In the adult world of the later works, the fall becomes not only an inevitable but also a necessary act of freedom; and those who consciously try to maintain their "white" innocence—like Nel or Macon Dead or Jadine— merit a condemnation spared the pathetic Pecola.

Once innocence gives way to experience, ignorance is never forgivable, we discover, however much one is oppressed by the viciousness of others. We can pity the weak, but we must distance ourselves from them, allowing them to carry the burden of our own fear and self-contempt. So it is that Claudia can look back upon her defeated friend Pecola, knowing full well that she and Frieda had "honed [their] egos on her," "cleansed [themselves] on her," and dumped on her the "waste . . . which she absorbed" (162–63). Though someone to be pitied, Pecola is no sentimental sop. Not Pecola herself, but her unknowing, her ignorance, her passivity merit our contempt. Because in her madness Pecola evades the full consequences of knowledge, she eludes judgment. The imaginary friend she talks to in her madness, the last parody of the Dick-and-Jane passage, will guard her from the truth. But as Linda Wagner rightly says of Pecola's conversation with her "friend," "There is no more emphatic scene of existential loneliness in contemporary literature, but it is a loneliness with no hint of self-knowledge as redemption."[10] Ultimately, Pecola serves as scapegoat without benefit of martyrdom, a hopeless rather than tragic character.

It is the other characters who must bear the full weight of knowledge. What judgment there is is left to Claudia, who knows that "the country was hostile to marigolds that year" when Pecola endured Cholly's ambiguous attempt to love her, "to touch her, envelop her, give something of himself to her" (163). Separated from an innocence Pecola cannot escape because of her madness, Claudia recognizes her own culpability, acknowledging

10. "Toni Morrison: Mastery of Narrative," in *Contemporary Women Writers*, ed. Catherine Rainwater and William J. Scheick (Lexington: University of Kentucky Press, 1985), 195. Keith Byerman labels Pecola a "grotesque Messiah; she gives the world not grace but the illusion of relief from intolerable circumstances. She is sacrificed so others may live with the perversion of reality" ("Intense Behaviors: The Use of the Grotesque in *The Bluest Eye* and *Eva's Man*," *CLA Journal* 25, no. 4 [1982]: 452).

her willingness finally to "say the victim had no right to live" (164). Claudia realizes that indeed "sometimes good looks like evil; sometimes evil looks like good," that it was the pariahs Maginot Line and above all Cholly who truly loved Pecola. Though living after the fall, she possesses a knowledge rendered impotent by gradual accommodation to the conditions of the society. Speaking long after the Breedlove family has dissolved, she anticipates Nel's situation at the end of *Sula*, coming to the truth "too late" to redeem her world.

SULA

SULA reintroduces the theme of lost innocence, but rather than tracing the rites of passage through the seasons of a fateful year, it records a lifetime of becoming from 1919 to 1968. "I was certainly interested in talking about black girlhood in *The Bluest Eye*," Morrison has acknowledged, "and not so interested in it in *Sula*. I wanted to move into the other part of their lives. That is, who do the Claudias and Friedas, those feisty little girls, grow up to be?"[1] The novel amplifies and enriches the theme of the fall, devoting half the narrative to recounting the main characters' existence after the fall. Set in the black neighborhood of Bottom before it became the Medallion City Golf Course "for whites only," it tells the story of a divided self projected in the lives of two girls-turned-women, who, rejecting the Other as part of the self, cannot resolve the duality which marks their fallen condition. Whereas Morrison depicts how Pecola Breedlove serves as the "other" against which Claudia, Frieda, and the black community measure themselves in *The Bluest Eye*, in *Sula* she centers full attention on the complementary relationship between Nel and Sula as a divided self. Their tragic alienation illustrates with increasing perception the potentially destructive consequences of innocence and the ambiguity of good and evil.

The idea of the double is one of those clichés Morrison has said she likes to "work with, to fret." The interrelated themes of the double, the Other, the shadow, the *Doppelgänger,* are of course long-standing in literature, but their roots lie deep in Romanticism. As Masao Miyoshi has noted, the idea of the divided self developed from the

1. Robert B. Stepto, "'Intimate Things in Place': A Conversation with Toni Morrison," in *Chant of Saints: A Gathering of Afro-American Literature, Art, and Scholarship*, ed. Michael S. Harper and Robert B. Stepto (Urbana: University of Illinois Press, 1979), 221.

26

collapse of Neoclassicism and the emergence of Gothicism and Romanticism in the late eighteenth century.[2] Morrison's adaptation of the motif, however, does not mirror the conventional use of the theme. She "frets" the cliché to delineate again the mythic fall of black characters caught in a hostile environment.

Nonetheless, Morrison's ideas do echo in large measure the post-Romantic conception of the fall. Since at least the appearance of *Faust*, the idea of the double has defined conflict in modern versions of the fall. In post-Romantic literature the most prevalent adaptation of the myth refers not to Adam and Eve so much as to Cain and Abel, to the Other's forbidden crime against his brother and rebellion against the established order. For the Romantics, the dark Other assumed heroic proportions. In such figures as Blake's Orcean revolutionary and Byron's Faustian hero, even in Shelley's demonic Count Cenci and perhaps Coleridge's enigmatic Geraldine, we witness the potentially restorative power of the opposing self who challenges the complementary figure's spiritually debilitating obedience to the system— Blake's "nobodaddy" god, Byron's tyrannical deity in *Cain*, the detached "Holy Father" and distant god in Shelley's *The Cenci*. There are of course later samples in American literature, and much modern fiction growing out of the Romantic concept of the divided self depicts the ambivalent forces of good and evil pitted against each other in creative tension, the figure of evil often assuming the nature of good, the figure of good revealing a capacity for evil. In the Romantic sense of a fortu-

2. *The Divided Self: A Perspective on the Literature of the Victorians* (New York: New York University Press, 1969). See Robert Rogers, *The Double in Literature* (Detroit: Wayne State University Press, 1970), for a psychological approach to the theme; Karl Miller, *Doubles: Studies in Literary History* (Oxford: Oxford University Press, 1986), for a wide-ranging historical treatment of the theme from Romantic to modern literature; H. M. Paleski, *The Divided Heroine: A Recurrent Pattern in Six English Novels* (New York: Holmes and Meier, 1984), for a study of "divided" female characters.

nate fall, the conflict proves both necessary and ambiguous. Indeed, the absence of conflict triggered by the Other would lead to that most frightening of Romantic ills—stasis.

Morrison's avowed intent "to confront a reality unlike the received reality of the West . . . to centralize and animate information discredited by the West" may explain her affinity for the Romantic version of the fall. The particular achievement of Morrison's adaptation of the fall myth is that by accommodating it in her larger vision, she is able to deconstruct the value system Western culture has tended to construct around it. Though not necessarily directly influenced by Romantic writers, she nonetheless embodies a vision common to theirs, but she infuses it with Afro-American myth, shaping it to describe the black experience in American culture. In her attempt "to subvert [the reader's] traditional comfort so that he may experience an unorthodox one," she clearly could find the Romantic view of the fortunate fall a compatible conception. In all her novels innocence assumes the nature of a crime against the self, and only by confronting and somehow assimilating the Other can Morrison's protagonists achieve a degree of existential freedom.

Sula becomes the contrary without which, as Blake wrote, "is no progression." Despite her dangerous potential, she provides the opportunity for Nel to throw off her "mind forg'd manacles," the self-protective innocence that denies her selfhood. It becomes the function of the other self to provide a dialectical pole, like Mephistopheles, and to goad the protagonist into action. Sula fulfills this role much as her male counterpart, Guitar Bains, does in *Song of Solomon*.

In an interview with Claudia Tate, Morrison has commented that she "really wasn't writing about" good and evil "in Western terms" in *Sula*. "It was interesting to me that black people at one time seemed not to respond to evil in the ways other people did," she remarked, "but that they thought evil had a natural place in the universe; they did not need to eradicate it. . . . Evil is not an alien force; it's just a different force."[3] She implies that good and evil coexist necessarily, a theory of opposites reflective of more Eastern or African than traditional Western thought. In such a view good devoid of evil soon leads to spiritual imbalance and moral entropy, and the terms good and evil all but cease to define moral categories or absolutes. Morrison has recalled, "In *Sula* I tried to posit a situation where there was a so-called good and a so-called evil people. Nel and Sula are symbolic of this situation. And, of course, you can't always tell which is which." She goes on to say that Nel and Sula "complement each other. They support each other. I suppose the two of them together would have made a wonderful single human being. But, you see, they are like a Janus head."[4] In tracing the evolving relationship between these characters, Morrison once again reveals the potential tyranny of innocence and the redemptive power of evil.

The novel is constructed upon opposites illustrating the paradoxical nature of good and evil. The "so-called good" and "so-called evil" people are first characterized by Helene Wright, Nel's self-righteous mother, and Eva Peace, Sula's remarkable grandmother. Nel's mother, Helene Sabat, had been born to a Creole whore in New Orleans and raised by her grandmother. Denying her affiliation with her real mother, Helene at seventeen married a ship's cook appropriately named "Wright" and moved to Medallion, near the Great Lakes. A formidable and proper woman, she joined the most conservative black church, wore her hair in a bun, and "won all social battles with presence and a conviction of the legitimacy of her authority."[5] When Nel was born nine years into the mar-

3. "Toni Morrison," in *Black Women Writers*, ed. Claudia Tate (New York: Continuum, 1983), 129.

4. Bettye J. Parker, "Complexity: Toni Morrison's Women—An Interview Essay," in *Sturdy Black Bridges: Visions of Black Women in Literature*, ed. Roseann P. Bell, Bettye J. Parker, and Beverly Guy-Sheftall (New York: Anchor Press/Doubleday, 1979), 253.

5. *Sula* (New York: Alfred A. Knopf, 1973), 18. Page numbers hereafter in parentheses in the text.

riage, Helene tried to negate her blackness, forcing her to pull her nose and put a clothespin on it to straighten it and to use a hot comb on Saturday night to straighten her hair. A legalist like Geraldine in *The Bluest Eye*, she "enjoyed manipulating her daughter and her husband" (18), and she equated whiteness with moral superiority.

The novel introduces Helene and Nel in 1920, when Helene's grandmother dies and she feels obligated to return for the funeral. She takes Nel with her on the long train ride. Humiliated by whites and forced to urinate in the woods because there are no restrooms for "coloreds," Helene suffers without protest during the train ride, at one point even smiling "dazzling and coquettishly" at the conductor, who tells her to "git [her] butt" in the car for coloreds. Only Nel sees the judgmental "midnight eyes" of two black soldiers who witness her mother's passive subservience. In New Orleans Helene tries to detach Nel from a world of prostitutes and garish sensuality, telling her pointedly that "I don't talk Creole . . . and neither do you" (27). Ashamed of her blackness, Helene Wright reveals the ironic guilt that Berndt Ostendorf characterizes in *Black Literature in White America*: "Shame cultural behavior is obvious in black culture in proportion to white cultural dominance: hair straighteners and skin bleachers are objectifications of a shame that runs deep in the unconscious."[6]

In contrast to Helene, one of the "so-called good people," Morrison offers the also appropriately named Eva Peace and Hannah, Sula's mother. Whereas the Wright home is always clean and sanitized, the Peace house has newspapers stacked in the doorway and dirty dishes. Nel wills to escape her mother's ordered home to find the warmth of the Peace house, where Eva hands out "goobers from deep within her pocket or [reads] you a dream" (29). Contrary to Nel's pious mother, Hannah is a "guileless" lover who "rippled with sex." Morrison once

6. *Black Literature in White America* (Totowa, New Jersey: Barnes & Noble, 1982), 31.

described her as "uncomplicated" and incapable of "jealousy or hostility." Childlike in her innocence and free of guilt, Hannah is not only tolerated by the women to whose husbands she makes love, but is also respected. They feel complimented that someone else wants their husbands. When she dies of burns, Morrison has commented, "the people in the town . . . miss her. . . . They take care of her when she burns and weep for her when she dies."[7]

Hannah's mother, Eva, is even more remarkable in her seeming amorality. Having been abandoned with three children after five years of marriage, she left Medallion for eighteen months and returned with only one leg. Some say she stuck her leg under a train to collect the insurance, but "whatever the fate of her lost leg, the remaining one was magnificent" (31). Living in her bizarre house with its oddly placed stairways, rooms, and doors, added over a thirty-five year period, she had brought up her three children: Hannah; Eva (called Pearl), who married and went off to Michigan; and Ralph (called Plum), who returned from the war shell-shocked and psychologically broken. A woman of mysterious power, Eva had taught her daughters "man-love" and, as Morrison has remarked, says "all the right things."[8]

An early incident establishing Morrison's theme of the ambiguity of good and evil concerns Eva's complicity in Plum's death. "[P]laying God," she burns to death her drunken and broken son when she realizes he wants to crawl back into her womb rather than function like a man. After first rocking him and loving him, she anoints him with kerosene, sets him aflame, and struggles painfully back to her upstairs room. Plum's death presents a parable of a fall—he could not return to the womb, to innocence.

7. Parker, "Complexity: Toni Morrison's Women—An Interview Essay," 254. In another interview Morrison has remarked, "Oh Hannah, the mother—I tell you, I think I felt more affection for her than anybody else in that book. I just loved her" (Stepto, "'Intimate Things in Place,'" 218).
8. Parker, "Complexity: Toni Morrison's Women—An Interview Essay," 255.

In his pitiable Oedipal state, Plum tries to arrest time, but Eva knows that he cannot exist in stasis. His ritual death manifests Eva's power as what Barbara Christian calls a "primeval Earth Mother Goddess"; she "both gives life and takes it away. She performs a ritual killing inspired by love—a ritual of sacrifice by fire." Yet, as Christian and others have concluded, Eva pays the price for her violent love when she cannot save the innocent Hannah from subsequent death by fire.[9] In events as in characters, Morrison reiterates that good and evil indeed often look like each other.

The first half of the novel recounts Nel and Sula's initiation into a world of moral inversion like Pecola's. Here Sula, like the serpent her birthmark sometimes represents, challenges the arrested innocence guarded by Nel's mother. She fulfills Nel's will to be free of Helene's smothering goodness, a desire Nel first expresses on the trip to New Orleans. Nel had "felt both pleased and ashamed" to witness the "stricken" look of the two black soldiers on the train when they saw Helene's "dazzling smile" at the racist conductor. Their "bubbling hatred" manifests something of her own unconscious desire. And when she returns to Medallion, she stares at her mirror in open rebellion:

"I'm me," she whispered. "Me."
Nel didn't quite know what she meant but on the other hand she knew exactly what she meant.
"I'm me. I'm not their daughter. I'm not Nel. I'm me. Me." (28)

9. *Black Women Novelists: The Development of a Tradition, 1892–1976* (Westport, Conn.: Greenwood Press, 1980), 159–60; see also Keith Byerman, *Fingering the Jagged Grain: Tradition and Form in Recent Black Fiction* (Athens: University of Georgia Press, 1985), 159. Morrison told Jane Bakerman, "Parents who simply adore their children and really and truly want the best for them may, in fact, destroy them. They say to them, as Eva did, 'Your life is not worth living'" ("The Seams Can't Show: An Interview with Toni Morrison," *Black American Literature Forum* 12 [1978]: 60).

Morrison concludes, "The trip, perhaps, or her new found me-ness, gave her strength to cultivate a friend in spite of her mother" (29).

If Helene drives "her daughter's imagination underground," Sula animates Nel's will to power. She becomes the Other and fulfills the role attributed to the "double" by Karl Miller: "One self does what the other self can't. One self is meek while the other is fierce." Sula articulates what Miller calls "the rule of contraries, which is another name for the double, with its constant inversions and reversals."[10] Sula and Nel form a whole, Morrison suggests in the novel: "they found in each other's eyes the intimacy they were looking for" (52). One light skinned, living in a tidy and respectable house, daughter of a fastidious and pious woman, the other "heavy brown," living in a disreputable and chaotic house, daughter of a loose woman, Nel and Sula instinctively forge an alliance, an "unconscious sympathy" not uncommon in post-Romantic literature. Though ostensibly contraries, they are, Blake might say, not "negatives." That is, they "are very much alike," according to Morrison. "They complement each other. They support each other."[11] Their relationship recalls other Romantic and post-Romantic pairs of opposites—Christabel and Geraldine, for example.[12] "They themselves [have] difficulty distinguishing one's thought from the other's" (83). Nel admits after her bitter separation from Sula that "Talking to Sula had always been a conversation with herself" (95). Significantly, their relationship, similar to that between Pecola and Claudia and her sister, begins when Nel is ten and in search of identity, yearning to escape the spurious innocence Helene has tried futilely to protect.

As a pole in the central dialectic, Sula represents the

10. *Doubles: Studies in Literary History*, 415.

11. Parker, "Complexity: Toni Morrison's Women—An Interview Essay," 253.

12. Chikwenye Okojo Ogunyemi especially notes the parallels with Leggatt and the Captain in Conrad's "The Secret Sharer" ("*Sula*: 'A Nigger Joke,'" *Black American Literature Forum* 13, no. 4 [1979]: 131–33).

dark unconscious, the "evil" underside of the imagination—what Morrison has labeled "a classic type of evil
force," yet not "freakish or repulsive or unattractive."[13]
Nel finds her both necessary and frightening. Drawn to
her, she nonetheless cannot fully acknowledge or compre-
hend her Other, guarding herself from Sula's awesome
will. Recalling an incident when Sula cut off the tip of her
finger to frighten four white boys who threatened the
girlfriends, Nel claims that "Sula was so scared she had
mutilated herself, to protect herself" (101). But in fact, Sula
did not engage in the blood ritual to protect only herself
but Nel as well. Furthermore, she was not "scared"—she
decided that she and Nel would go home via the route
where she knew they would meet the white boys, she
intentionally brought along the house knife, and she
showed no fear whatever when accosted. Yet Morrison
has said Nel and Sula counterbalance each other. They
exist in tenuous balance as they grow to womanhood—
Nel leans on Sula, and Sula seeks reassurance in Nel's
ordered world. They together share the loss of innocence
in a series of experiences in 1922 when they are both
twelve, the age of accountability.

Morrison begins the section "1922" with the blood ritual
noted above and follows it with key initiations. By this
time Nel is "no longer interested" in straightening her
hair with "the hateful hot comb," and both she and Sula
strike a new theme—"men." They secretly rejoice when
Ajax calls them "Pig meat," and "smooth vanilla
crotches" of the young black men invite them (50). At this
point of heightened sensitivity, Sula suffers a first rite of
passage when she overhears Hannah say that she loves
Sula but does not "like her" (57). Running to her room
while "aware of a sting in her eye," she finds herself
alienated, rejected by her mother like the far weaker
Pecola Breedlove. She experiences the "dark thoughts" of
a new awareness until Nel comes to find her. Their escape

13. Stepto, "'Intimate Things in Place,'" 215.

34

into the bright summer day leads to shared events marking the culmination of their childhood. Morrison introduces the first occurrence with a wonderfully sensitive passage describing Nel and Sula freely running together by the river, flinging "themselves into the four-cornered shade to taste their lip sweat." On the edge of sexual awakening, "their small breasts just . . . beginning to create some pleasant discomfort when they were lying on their stomachs" (58), the two act out "[i]n concert" the symbolic burial of their childhood and foreshadow a demonic if unwitting will to power. They each begin to "undress" a twig by stripping it down to "a smooth creamy innocence" and begin stroking the ground until Nel makes "a small neat hole that grew deeper and wider with the least manipulation of her twig" (58). Sula copies her until they make the two holes "one and the same." When Nel's twig breaks, she begins burying it in the hole:

> Sula threw hers in too. Nel saw a bottle cap and tossed it in as well. Each then looked around for more debris to throw into the hole: paper, bits of grass, butts of cigarettes, until all of the small defiling things they could find were collected there. Carefully they replaced the soil and covered the entire grave with uprooted grass. Neither one had spoken a word. (58–59)

This richly sexual moment signals their imminent passage into experience, their joint fall from childlike innocence. It occurs when Sula tempts the recently arrived boy Chicken Little to climb a tree by the river.

When she helps him down, Sula begins playfully swinging Chicken around and around—until he slips from her hands and lands in the river. Neither Sula nor Nel reacts. They watch Chicken sink into the river. Guilty, they stare at the darkened water, no longer able to claim innocence. Ironically, Nel tells the nearly hysterical Sula, "You didn't mean to. It ain't your fault" (62–63), trying to preserve an innocence she has herself lost. Although Nel knows she has "done nothing," she feels "convicted and hanged" (65).[14] Philip A. Royster makes the important observation that though Nel herself does not recognize it, it is she and not Sula who taunts Chicken, revealing a sadistic pleasure she can only confess long after Sula's death.[15] Indeed, only at the end of the novel can Nel understand that there is no innocence.

As Nel and Sula leave Chicken's funeral, they walk home with "their fingers . . . laced in as gentle a clasp as that of any two young girlfriends trotting up the road on a summer day wondering what happened to butterflies in the winter" (66). The girls unwittingly emerge from childhood—indeed, they are already two butterflies in winter—while ironically, the adults at Chicken's funeral can see "the truly innocent child hiding in the corner of their hearts" and suffer "the oldest and most devastating pain there is: not the pain of childhood, but the remembrance of it" (65).

So long as they somehow share their experiences, the girls maintain the equilibrium that secures their wholeness, but as Morrison has explained, "the loss of their friendship, which is actually the balance wheel for each woman," triggers their failure to reconcile the contrary

14. Chikwenye Okojo Ogunyemi argues that the death of Chicken Little "serves as a point of separation between the two girls from a moral perspective." Sula, he contends, "weeps hysterically," whereas Nel is calm, less concerned about the tragic occurrence than about the possible detection of the crime. Shadrack, the shell-shocked soldier who returned to Bottom from World War I and established National Suicide Day, had apparently witnessed the drowning. Nel, according to Ogunyemi, was upset with Sula because she left her belt in Shadrack's cabin when she went to look for him. He concludes that "to Nel the truth can always be camouflaged" ("Sula: 'A Nigger Joke,'" 31). At this point, though, Nel seems neither cunning nor condemnatory. Not until later does she consciously protect her innocence.

15. "A Priest and a Witch against The Spiders and Snakes: Scapegoating in Toni Morrison's *Sula*," *Umoja* 2 (1978): 154–55. Barbara Hill Rigney offers a feminist reading, calling Chicken's death "the ritualized sacrifice of the male child" following "a parody of the kind of defloration ritual common in matriarchal cultures" (*Lilith's Daughters: Women and Religion in Contemporary Fiction* [Madison: University of Wisconsin Press, 1982], 62–63).

forces of good and evil in themselves.[16] On the day five years later when Nel marries Jude, "a handsome well-liked bridegroom," Sula leaves for a period of ten years. Until her marriage, Nel could only escape her stern repressive parents through Sula. For a decade in Sula's absence, Nel begins to create her own specious garden, where she raises her children and gradually begins to recreate the "oppressive neatness" of her mother's home. Middle class conventionality and a dull sameness form her life. Even her love for Jude "had cooked out . . . like a pan of syrup kept too long on the stove" (165). When Sula returns, marking the second half of the novel, Nel at first welcomes her, "like getting the use of an eye back, having a cataract removed" (95), only to see her joy transformed into fear. Sula seems a presence of evil, the serpent who challenges Nel's existential stasis. Now part of a divided self, Sula becomes the demonic power in Nel's life, generating an inevitable struggle between seeming opposites, much like Guitar Bains becomes the shadow figure haunting Milkman Dead in *Song of Solomon*.

When Claudia Tate suggested to Morrison that Cholly Breedlove, Guitar Bains, Ajax and Sula "are golden-eyed people, the dangerously free people," Morrison went on to say that "they express either an effort of the will or a freedom of the will. . . . There's a wildness that they have, a nice wildness. . . . It's pre-Christ in the best sense. It's Eve. When I see this wildness gone in a person, it's sad."[17] Sula assumes the nature of the free black man, an Eve driven by "tremendous curiosity" to run the risk of freedom. She has something in common with the traditional Romantic villain, the character whose seeming "evil" generates good. Having already demonstrated a capacity for evil, as when she watches her own mother burn to death, Sula returns to play the role of the outsider, arriving amid a plague of dead robins and other signs of metaphysical disorder.

16. Bakerman, "The Seams Can't Show," 60.
17. Tate, "Toni Morrison," 125–26.

And Bottom is very much in need of resurrection. Sula herself recognizes the sorry state of the women in the village:

> . . . she [sees] how the years [have] dusted their bronze with ash, the eyes that [have] opened wide to the moon bent into growing sickles of concern. The narrower their lives, the wider their hips. Those with husbands [have] folded themselves into starched coffins, their sides bursting with other people's skinned dreams and bony regrets. (121–22)

Despite their condemnation of Sula, the women allow her to claim her place in the community and tolerate her outrageous behavior, in part to excuse and exorcise an "evil" buried in themselves. Morrison has pronounced Sula's return "a triumphant thing and not a defeat" and has observed that though Sula is a pariah to the community, she is "nevertheless protected there as she would not be elsewhere."[18] To the black community, evil has always had a claim of legitimacy, she notes. After all, "they know God had a brother and that brother hadn't spared God's son, so why should he spare them?" (118). But also, Sula expresses that "evil" which is part of them all, that Eve-like will to be free from their narrow existence. Paradoxically, rather than threatening their moral consciousness, her presence revitalizes it, coercing them "to protect and love one another," "to cherish their husbands and wives, protect their children, repair their homes" (117). Whatever her evil, Sula offers a redemptive power.

At first Nel embraces Sula's regenerating spirit, so that

> . . . the dishes piled in the sink [look] as though they [belong] there; the dust on the lamps [sparkles]: the hair brush lying on the "good" sofa in the living room [does] not have to be apologetically retrieved, and Nel's grimy intractable children [look] like three wild things happily insouciant in the May shine. (96)

18. Nellie McKay, "An Interview with Toni Morrison," *Contemporary Literature* 24, no. 4 (1983): 425–26.

The passage echoes the early descriptions of the chaotic Peace household, and the children recall the three Deweys whom Eva had raised without the least regard for propriety or discipline. But Sula invades as much as enlivens Nel's world, and she ironically convinces Nel to help secure Eva Peace's insurance money and put her in a disreputable home. More, she seduces Jude, apparently without remorse or even consciousness that it will cause Nel pain. She has already made love to and discarded others' husbands. Having "no center around which to grow. . . . She is completely free of ambition," Morrison has remarked, "with no affection for money, property or things, no greed, no desire to command attention or compliments—no ego."[19] Amoral and so without conscience, she stands beyond judgment.

Sula feels remorse only for a lost innocence, even when making love to any husband who happened to appeal to her: "She wept then. Tears for the deaths of the littlest things: the castaway shoes of children; broken stems of marsh grass battered and drowned by the sea; prom photographs of dead women she never knew; wedding rings in pawnshop windows; the tiny bodies of Cornish hens in a nest of rice" (123). In consequence of her fall from innocence to experience, she is profoundly aware of time and "a loneliness so profound the word itself [has] no meaning" (123). Her freedom from the community that Nel comes to represent, as all freedom, comes at enormous cost. Caught in a tragic dilemma, she chooses freedom only at the cost of the Other, the side of her self projected by Nel. That is why her relationship with Ajax cannot endure. The "dangerously free" Ajax is Jude's opposite. Jude had married Nel to be a mother to him, "to care about his hurt, to care very deeply." Denied jobs by the white establishment, he had sought "to take on a man's role" by marrying Nel, intending to make the two of them "one Jude" (82–83). But Ajax wants no proof of his manhood, needs no sign of his worthiness to compete with whites,

19. Tate, "Toni Morrison," 119.

enters no contracts to legalize his selfhood. So when Sula, behaving like Nel, does "a little number with the dishes and cleans up her house and puts on a ribbon in her hair," as Morrison has said, Ajax "detected the scent of the nest."[20] As all fall stories tell us, Sula cannot build garden walls and also live in freedom.

She intends no harm to Nel, believing her a "version of herself which she [seeks] to reach out and touch with an ungloved hand," so she is surprised by Nel's rejection, suddenly realizing that Nel has become "one of *Them*," part of "the town and all its ways" (120). Afraid of "the flick of their tongues" and guarding her garden, Nel resorts to being Helene Wright once more, holding tenaciously to her security. Sula thinks of her as a spider suspended by its own spittle over a waiting snake below, "more terrified by the free fall than the snake's breath" (120). This passage is anticipated by Morrison's earlier remark that Nel's love for Jude "over the years had spun a steady grey web around her heart" (95). If Nel's marriage makes her a legitimate part of the community, Jude's betrayal necessitates a reassertion of her place. Unwilling to run the risk of a fall, Nel knows "how to behave as the wronged wife" (120), wrapping the drapery of her innocence about her like the other women who have "folded themselves into starched coffins." Having given up her individuality in marriage, she opts again to deny the other self. Fearful of risking a fall, Nel defines hell as change, whereas Sula, the demonic risk-taker, defines hell as "doing anything forever and ever" (108). Nel cannot leave the security Sula considers an existential hell, choosing like Pauline Breedlove and Geraldine to maintain the fortress of her innocence. She uses Sula as Pauline uses Cholly to maintain her self-righteousness.

Later, when Sula is dying, significantly reenacting in her memory "the digging of two holes" when she and Nel ritualistically buried their childhood, she instinctively

20. Parker, "Complexity: Toni Morrison's Women—An Interview Essay," 254.

40

reaches out one last time to her Other—"Wait'll I tell Nel" (149). Even then she is the agent of experience. Having "sung all the songs there are," she reverts to a childlike innocence, reenters the womb as Plum tried to do, curled like a fetus with her thumb in her mouth, and experiences death "completely alone—where she had always wanted to be" (148). Yet even then she wills to tell Nel what it is like to die. As Sula is unable to be free of Nel even in death, Nel cannot disengage herself from Sula or the "evil" her Other bears as scapegoat.

Although Sula separated from Nel becomes a demonic force set loose in the community, she once told Eva Peace that she had come back to resurrect life in the dead village. In fact, at her death "a falling away" takes place. "Now that Sula [is] dead and done with," the community suffers "dislocation" (153). A bitter October ice storm leads to a dismal Thanksgiving, and an epidemic of croup and scarlet fever follows. Tea Pot's mother, who had stopped abusing him when she saw Sula helping him up after he fell outside the house, begins to beat him again, and other mothers resume abusing their children. The rumor that blacks will be hired to build the tunnel again proves false. Daughters return "to steeping resentment of the burdens of old people. Wives [uncoddle] their husbands . . . and even those Negroes who had moved down from Canada . . . [return] to their original claims of superiority" (153–54). The disintegration of the community culminates on National Suicide Day when Shadrack leads much of the populace on a death march he had first announced on January 3, 1920. The communal death is the manifestation of a community already dying, where, Sula has told Nel, "every colored woman in the country" is dying, and where the white community has already begun to invade the land and invert its values. A fall and death occurs in every section of the novel, and the tunnel deaths are the ultimate judgment on a lost people whose celebration of Sula's death is merely an announcement of their own. Bottom is destroyed from within, a paradise already ruined by self-possessiveness and moral certainty. The tunnel becomes a communal womb, a perverse symbol of aborted life. Suggestively, it is also a tunnel constructed by whites.

Nel alone comes to understand Sula's regenerative power. Before Sula's return had compelled her into action by disrupting her sterile garden, Nel had lapsed into an easy accommodation. Forced by Sula to choose between moral absolutism and freedom with all its risks, Nel has clung to her innocence, repressing the side of herself that Sula mirrors like the prototypal serpent in Eden. Sula had vainly attempted to question her surety in their last conversation:

> She opened the door and heard Sula's low whisper. "Hey girl." Nel paused and turned her head but not enough to see her.
> "How you know?" Sula asked.
> "Know what?" Nel still wouldn't look at her.
> "About who was good. How do you know it was you?"
> "What you mean?"
> "I mean maybe it wasn't you. Maybe it was me." (146)

Speaking of this scene, Morrison has observed that "living totally by the law and surrendering to it without questioning anything sometimes makes it impossible to know anything about yourself."[21] In 1940 Nel still hid behind her moral certitude.

And it is not until the end, twenty-five years after Sula's death, that Nel comes to recognize the evil of her good. Going to the graveyard where Eva Peace and her children lay buried, Nel in 1965 suddenly remembers how Sula cried and cried when Chicken Little drowned in 1922. She begins to realize that Sula had acted out her own unconscious demonic potential, that the crime is not Sula's alone: "That good feeling she had had when Chicken's hands had slipped. She hadn't wondered about that in years. 'Why didn't I feel bad when it happened? How come it felt so good to see him fall?'" (170).

21. Stepto, "'Intimate Things in Place,'" 216–17.

She too is part of fallen humanity. Indeed, at the home just before she dies, Eva Peace tells Nel, "You. Sula. What's the difference? You watched didn't you?" (168). Eva, who could commit the "crime" of burning to death her only son in a profound act of love and yet risk her own life trying to save her daughter from fire, experiences good and evil in human rather than moralistic terms. Her crime is paradoxically an act of compassion—and Nel's apparent innocence is nothing less than criminal. At last Nel comes to the ironic revelation that she has condemned herself in rejecting Sula: "'All that time, all that time, I thought I was missing Jude.' And the loss pressed down on her chest and came up into her throat. 'We were girls together,' she said as though explaining something. 'O Lord, Sula,' she cried 'girl, girl, girlgirlgirl'" (174). Having failed to acknowledge her other self, to forgive and so to embrace her, she has paid the price for her sin against herself. Her goodness has ravaged her humanity.

Morrison has spoken admiringly of Nel, acknowledging that she likes people who "do it"—"She will take care of the children and do the work . . . the bread will be there."[22] But clearly she sees a Nel without Sula as tragically deficient, tragically because Nel cannot hold to Sula without violating the legitimate demands of the community and conventional morality. Nel suffers because she accepts all claims of the community on her; Sula suffers because she accepts none. Either way leads to tragic choice. Sula's freedom and Nel's security constitute the conditions of tragedy. Morrison has admitted that she writes in "the tragic mode" and has explained the tragic paradox that underlies her fiction:

. . . a lot of people complain about my endings, because it

22. Parker, "Complexity: Toni Morrison's Women—An Interview Essay," 253. Elsewhere she has labeled Nel "one of those people you know are going to pay the gas bill and take care of the children. . . . And they are magnificent, because they take these small tasks and they do them" (Stepto, "'Intimate Things in Place,'" 215).

looks like they are falling apart. But something important has happened; some knowledge is there—the Greek knowledge—what is the epiphany in Greek tragedy. . . . It can't be undone. And in that sense it is Greek in the sense that the best you can hope for is some realization and that, you know, a certain amount of suffering is not just anxiety.[23]

What she describes are the consequences of a fall, the painful but tragically victorious journey east of Eden that Nel can begin once she is armed with the knowledge of good and evil in herself. Keith E. Byerman has best defined the end of the novel: "Thus Eva, like her namesake, forces on another knowledge of good and evil and thereby brings Nel out of her self-created innocence into a world of history, experience, and responsibility. The mark of this fortunate fall is her embrace of the spirit of Sula."[24] Nel's "victory" is no more than the suffering paid for a final truth—that there is no innocence after knowledge. And perhaps that is enough. One truth we know: as one of the characters in Robert Heinlein's *Stranger in a Strange Land* remarks, "Innocence is not enough. Innocence is never enough."

23. Bessie W. Jones, "An Interview with Toni Morrison," in Bessie W. Jones and Audrey L. Vinson, *The World of Toni Morrison* (Dubuque, Iowa: Kendall/Hunt, 1985), 136.

24. *Fingering the Jagged Grain*, 200.

SONG OF SOLOMON

MORRISON'S third novel shifts from a rural setting, emphasizing the pronounced racial dislocation of blacks transported from a nature-bound community to the more materialistic dominance of white urban culture. It is no accident that Milkman Dead is the first black born in Southside Mercy Hospital or that his birth is triggered ironically by the fall of the black life insurance agent Robert Smith. Both signal the dismemberment of the black community. Milkman is born in the very hospital where his deceased Uncle Tom grandfather, Dr. Foster, could not send his black patients. His birth there suggests not so much a victory for blacks as evidence of the white control of his life. And it is from the cupola of what blacks fittingly called "No Mercy Hospital" that Robert Smith tries in vain to escape the dismal failure of blacks to defeat the tyranny of an unjust system. His "fall" results from a lack of faith in himself, a truth acknowledged when he writes "Please forgive me" on the note tacked to his door, an admission that he cannot believe in himself. Unredeemed by self-forgiveness, he learns "that only birds and airplanes [can] fly."[1] But by the end of the novel Milkman Dead will realize that one "must fall to be free," that to fly you must first reclaim what Nietzsche called "the ground of being." Paradoxically, to fall and to fly become the same act as Milkman acknowledges when he "leaps" at his brother Guitar Bains in the conclusion of the novel.

Structurally more linear than *The Bluest Eye* or *Sula*, *Song of Solomon* divides into two sections: the larger portion recounts Milkman Dead's growing dissatisfaction in his father's urban Eden; the second section presents what several have described as the monomyth of the hero's

---

1. *Song of Solomon* (New York: Alfred A. Knopf, 1977), 9. Page numbers hereafter in parentheses in the text.

quest for identity.[2] Clearly, Milkman's journey to self-hood—his recovery of a racial past, his discovery of his true "home"—requires him to undergo unmistakable rites of passage that parallel the stages of the fortunate fall we have noted earlier. Under the influence of the snakelike Pilate and his Other, his friend Guitar Bains, he must leave his father's perverse garden; he must gain self-knowledge, suffer humiliation and shame, risk death to understand and resurrect his "dead" spirit. Morrison employs biblical themes, fairy tales, Afro-American myth, and classical myth to describe his fall. She charts these stages chronologically in the form of a *Bildungsroman* while maintaining as constant the ubiquitous presentness of the past that compels Milkman to act.

When Milkman at age four discovers that he cannot fly, he settles into the spiritual morass of his father's "white nigger" world. Forced to wear velvet suits to meet his parents' pretensions, he is ostracized by other blacks. The tyrannical father-god Macon Dead is "a nigger in business . . . a terrible thing to see," as Guitar Bains' grandmother tells her grandson when Macon refuses to give her more time to pay her rent. Being "already a colored man of property," Macon had married a sixteen-year-old, the only child of Dr. Foster, "just about the biggest Negro in the city." A reflection of the materialistic white power structure, Macon preaches his gospel to his son: "Let me tell you right now the one important thing you'll ever need to know: Own things. And let the things you own own other things. Then you'll own yourself and other people too" (55).

Milkman's mother is another of those women, like Helene Wright and Geraldine, who imitate bourgeois whites,

2. See especially Leslie Harris, "Myth as Structure in Toni Morrison's *Song of Solomon*," *MELUS* 7, no. 3 (1980): 69–76; Charles DeArman, "Milkman as the Archetypal Hero: 'Thursday's child has to go,'" *Obsidian* 6, no. 3 (1980): 56–59; Dorothy H. Lee, "*Song of Solomon*: To Ride the Air," *Black American Literature Forum* 16, no. 2 (1982): 64–70; and Wilfred D. Samuels, "Liminality and the Search for Self in Toni Morrison's *Song of Solomon*," *Minority Voices: An Interdisciplinary Journal of Literature and Art* 5, nos. 1/2 (1981): 59–68.

but she is more significantly a victim of her father's greed and arrogance. Dr. Foster's materialistic values had alienated him from his love-starved daughter as well as the black community he supposedly served. Macon tells his son that Dr. Foster, though "worshipped" like a god, called the poor blacks "cannibals" and lived in haughty splendor on the edge of the white neighborhood. His relationship with his daughter, Ruth, became increasingly embarrassing after his wife's death. Even at sixteen she insisted that he sit on her bed and "plant a kiss on her lips" each night, and she responded with "an ecstacy inappropriate to the occasion" (23). Macon objected when Ruth insisted that her father should deliver her two daughters—"She had her legs wide open and he was there" (71). More, he informs Milkman, though Ruth denied it, he found her naked in the bed with her dead father, "his fingers in her mouth" (73). He even admitted his fear that Lena and First Corinthians might not have been his own children. Psychologically twisted by the cold indifference of her power-driven father, Ruth apparently expresses an Electra complex. Milkman seems to think so when he follows her late one night to the cemetery where her father is buried and learns that six or seven times a year she would go to "lay down" on her father's grave (123). Denied access to her father and deserted by Macon, who refused to sleep with her after finding her in bed with her dead father, Ruth seeks some way to substitute for lost love. When Milkman was born through the witchlike powers of Pilate, Ruth nursed him until he was four. At least once a day she "unbuttoned her blouse and smiled" and entered "into fantasy," "staring not so much from maternal joy as from a wish to avoid seeing his legs dangling almost to the floor" (13).

Brought up by parents disenfranchised from other blacks and severely warped by the crass materialism they shared with the white power structure, Milkman, like Nel Wright, unconsciously seeks his double. Guitar Bains arouses Milkman's will to freedom as Sula does when she drives Nel from Helene Wright's spurious garden.

Identified with the dark and forbidden, like Sula Peace, Guitar assaults the "legitimate" world of Macon Dead. Befriending Milkman when the young Dead is twelve, the same formative age at which Sula befriends Nel, Guitar first introduces Milkman to his outcast Aunt Pilate. Just as Eva Peace's home is the opposite of Nel Wright's proper house, Pilate's is the reverse of the twelve-room, mortuarylike Foster house, where Macon keeps the Packard that blacks refer to as "the hearse." A bootleg store, it smells of earth and the fecundity of nature; it is a natural paradise set against the sterility of Macon Dead's house. Identified with nature, with trees, fruit, and eggs, Pilate is like Eve, a nurturer of life. And like "the mother of all living," Pilate even lacks a navel. She is what Morrison has called an "Ancestor," a "social or secret outlaw" who "must defy the system . . . provide alternate wisdom, and establish and maintain and sustain generations in the land."[3] Pilate functions along with Guitar as the serpent in Macon Dead's oppressive empire, itself a reflection of decadent white urban society. Threatening Milkman's power-possessed father and his capitalistic value system, Pilate is Milkman's true spiritual mother (Ruth is indeed a "Foster" mother): her magical potion made possible his birth; her curse protected him from Macon's attempts to have him aborted. She is the ancestor without whom Milkman has no true self, and she alone can ultimately shatter Macon's protective paradise.

Guitar Bains' first consequential act to free Milkman occurs, therefore, when he takes the twelve-year-old Milkman to his aunt's "notorious wine house." Milkman feels shame at meeting her, not shame about her, not shame because she was "ugly, dirty, poor, and drunk" or

3. "City Limits, Village Values: Concepts of the Neighborhood in Black Fiction," in *Literature & the Urban Experience: Essays on the City and Literature*, ed. Michael C. Jaye and Ann Chalmers Watts (New Brunswick, N.J.: Rutgers University Press, 1981), 43. See also Toni Morrison, "Rootedness: The Ancestor as Foundation," in *Black Women Writers (1950–1980): A Critical Evaluation*, ed. Mari Evans (Garden City, N.Y.: Anchor Press/Doubleday, 1984), 339–45.

"because he personally felt responsible for her ugliness, her poverty, her dirt, and her wine" (37–38). Rather, his shame comes from the realization that she is "unkempt" but not dirty, that although "she was anything but pretty . . . he knew he could watch her all day" (38). For the first time he feels shame for sinning against himself, not against his father. For the first time he feels "completely happy" being with Pilate and her daughter and granddaughter, Reb and Hagar, and is excited by the very act of disobeying his father's law. Yet even when he rejoices in Pilate's home and falls in love with Hagar, he is bound by Macon's rule. Ironically, Macon is "delighted" with Milkman because he is certain his fourteen-year-old son "[belongs] to him now" (63). He makes Milkman a conspirator in his oppression of blacks, using his son to collect rents for his shoddy tenements.

For sixteen or seventeen years Milkman tries to live a divided life, unable to commit himself. He flees to Pilate's house to make love to Hagar but also fulfills his role as his father's agent. Existing in spiritual stasis, unwilling or unable to commit a saving sin, he acts only once to assert his independence. With strong Oedipal impulses he knocks his father into the radiator when Macon strikes Ruth for a harmless social offense. Already walking with a limp, probably an allusion to the Oedipal myth, he challenges "the King of the Mountain." Twenty-two at the time, Milkman "felt glee. A snorting, horse-galloping glee as old as desire. He had won something and lost something in the same instant" (68). What he gains is a first measure of freedom; what he loses is the security of the garden. Because of Milkman's defiance, Macon tells him his account of Ruth's seeming perversity, but Milkman does not want the consequences of a fall, of freedom. He does not want knowledge, nor is he willing to assume the "enormous responsibilities" of freedom: "he was not prepared to take advantage of the former, or accept the burden of the latter" (68). Though Macon himself cannot confront the "whole truth," he rightly tells his son that "if you want to be a whole man, you have to deal with the whole truth" (70). Trying to wash his hands of knowledge ("What the fuck did he tell me that shit for?" [76]), Milkman retreats to a life bereft of meaning or responsibility. Even at thirty when he recalls striking his father as the only time he "acted independently," he opts to do "nothing," to evade "unwanted knowledge . . . as well as some responsibility for that knowledge" (120). The price of freedom is too great, so he steps back from the boundary wall of the garden to a "lazy righteousness." Like Nel Wright after her trip to New Orleans when she secretly rejoices in her mother's humiliation and seeks her own identity, Milkman stands before a mirror, but he lacks the courage to be. Once again it is Guitar who goads him and articulates self-judgment, just as Sula does for Nel.

Like Sula, Guitar functions as a pole in the dialectic, drawing Milkman from the control of his "white man" father. Charles Scruggs has suggested that when Macon Dead kills the old white man in the cave where he and Pilate had hidden to evade their father's killers, Macon becomes "the person he killed: a white man hoarding gold." For the rest of his life, Macon continues to live in "Mammon's Cave."[4] Though both Guitar and Macon's fathers experience hideous deaths exposing the rapaciousness of whites, the two sons respond in opposite but equally degenerate ways. One succumbs to violence and death in total disregard of the materialistic system; the other tries to accumulate wealth. Both teach Milkman something of truth—and both point him toward destruction.

As ruler of the Dead house, Macon controls Milkman's life, "blesses" him with ill-gotten wealth, and directs his life. When Milkman plots with Guitar to steal Pilate's "inheritance," the supposed sack of gold taken from the cave in Pennsylvania, he dreams of "boats, cars, airplanes, and the command of a large view." Guitar sym-

4. "The Nature of Desire in Toni Morrison's *Song of Solomon*," *Arizona Quarterly* 38, no. 4 (1982): 319.

bolically derides his values when he describes the "white faggot" peacock on the roof of the Nelson Buick building: "Too much tail. All that jewelry weighs it down. . . . Like vanity. Can't nobody fly with all that shit. Wanna fly you got to give up the shit that weighs you down" (179). Though dehumanized and debased by uncompromising hostility to anything "white," Guitar rightly judges Milkman guilty of thoughtless obedience to a repressive system. Incapable of anything but absolute hatred of whites, he would nonetheless have used the money stolen from Pilate to buy a marker for his father's grave and "stuff for his brothers and sisters, and his sisters' children" (179). When Milkman tells about his dream that his mother is being smothered by tulips (the victim of her prolonged life in the garden), Guitar accuses him of not helping her. And Milkman has to confess that "he didn't concern himself an awful lot about other people" (107). And indeed he cruelly abandons the devoted if possessive Hagar, thoughtlessly destroys his sister Corinthian's hope for happiness by telling Macon about her secret affair with Henry Porter, and washes his hands of any responsibility for racial injustice. Whatever his distorted views, Guitar rightly condemns Milkman's placidity and prods him to search for an authentic self.

Guitar, Leslie Harris has perceptively concluded, "is not so much Milkman's opposite as his double, an extension of the very negations Milkman has practiced." In finding his only brotherhood in the murderous Seven Days, she argues, he rejects all human ties just as Milkman spurns his family and Hagar. "Guitar's total commitment to death" in his association with the Seven Days "is only the logical extension of Milkman's attempt to fly away."[5] Put another way, Milkman wants freedom but without risk. He realizes finally that "there [is] nothing he [wants] bad enough to risk anything for, inconveniencing himself for" (107). As he himself had punned about his father, "He was already Dead." If Guitar represents a

5. "Myth as Structure in Toni Morrison's *Song of Solomon*," 74–75.

spiritual death by violence, Milkman symbolizes death by stasis. Yet, paradoxically, he knows he is dead and yearns to leave Not Doctor Street and hear the click of the house lock "settle into its groove for the last time" (163). Instinctively, he senses the danger of being destroyed like his mother, who is so bound by her allegiance to her father that her innocence turns into a smothering pile of tulips. He recognizes the falsity of his life and, like all who endure dissatisfaction in the garden, wants to leave. He fears spending "the rest of his life" doing Macon's work. He knows his life to be "a one-way street," "pointless, aimless" (107). He feels "off center" but wants "to know as little as possible," even though Pilate tells Ruth that if anything kills Milkman it will be "his own ignorance" (140).

When he is about to set off for Pennsylvania to trace the missing gold where Macon and Pilate first found it in the cave, he tells Guitar, "I don't want to be my father's office boy no more" (222). Disdainful of his father's world, he still half desires to remain in its safe confines, considers marrying a woman from the "Honoré crowd" and settling into a comfortable bourgeois life. He confides in Guitar not because he needs his help in acquiring the gold, but because his friend can "create the sense of danger and life lived on the cutting edge." He really wants something to free him from the gray and moribund Dead household and "from his parents' past, which [is] also their present and which [is] threatening to become his present as well" (180). In truth he wants a parasitic life, wants "to know as little as possible" and yet escape the sterility of his existence.

But while Guitar functions as the Other whom Milkman must accommodate to achieve a whole self, Pilate serves as the integrating center. At one extreme, Guitar rejects her for her "Aunt Jemima act" in front of the policemen who arrest Milkman and him for stealing Pilate's sack of bones. More, he accuses her of "crazy self-punishment" because she feels morally responsible for the death of the old white man in the cave. She insists that she "was part of her brother's act, because, then, she and he were one" (147). Her dead papa had told her "You just can't fly on off and leave a body," so she assumes he was commanding her to retrieve the dead man's bones because "if you take a life, then you own it. You responsible for it" (208). Given his moral indifference and unequivocal hatred of all whites, Guitar condemns Pilate absolutely.

At the other extreme, Macon denies her for opposite reasons. Though "he and she were one" until Pilate chased him from the cave for wanting to steal the gold, Macon sees her as a continuing threat to his white man paradise. When she suddenly appeared and tried to heal the breach between Ruth and him, he resented her. He finally chased her from the Dead house, where she cared for Milkman, because she showed no "respect for herself" and was a constant embarrassment. "That woman's no good," he now warns Milkman. "She's a snake and can charm you like a snake, but still a snake" (54). Judged guilty in light of Guitar's dehumanizing absolutism and Macon's respectable, white bourgeois values, Pilate alone can rescue Milkman. Charles Scruggs poses the interesting argument that as one denied "a community" by her brother, Pilate has become "an Eve without a garden."[6] Truly she is a nurturer of life and is marked with Eve's smooth stomach, but she is also what Macon fears, a serpent, a trickster who, while invading his little paradise, serves in the mythic role as healer and as catalyst to knowledge. Morrison has commented that the greatest danger in black urban culture is the demise of the "ancestor"—"if we don't keep in touch with the ancestor . . . we are, in fact, lost."[7] Pilate is the ancestor turned serpent in a spiritually impotent society.

Even when she first meets the near adolescent Milkman after being denied access to him for twelve years, Pilate challenges his secure but flawed world. She as-

6. "The Nature of Desire in Toni Morrison's *Song of Solomon*," 321.

7. "Rootedness: The Ancestor as Foundation," 344.

saults his assumptions and tries "to expel him from the very special group, in which he not only belonged, but had exclusive rights" (38–39). Ultimately, her "inheritance," the green Easter-egg sack hanging from the ceiling, is to be his own inheritance from the ancestor: "like Easter, it promised everything: the Risen Son and the heart's lone desire" (185). Significantly, when he and Guitar steal the sack, Milkman sees "the figure of a man standing right behind his friend" (186). Unwittingly eating of the fruit of knowledge, Milkman is to gain the self-awareness inherent in the fall. The image of the man is the first evidence of his contact with the spiritual power of a past rendered dormant in an alien home. The ghostly figure, like the black apparitions that later haunt Jadine in *Tar Baby*, marks the emergence of racial consciousness.

The shame Milkman feels after watching Pilate play her "Aunt Jemina act" marks a turning point in the novel. It drives a wedge between him and Guitar, and it signals a shift in the direction of Milkman's journey toward selfhood. The break with Guitar comes from Milkman's larger vision, his awareness that Pilate has once again sacrificed herself for him. The shame he had felt when he knocked Macon against the radiator, the "shame of seeing his father crumple before any man—even himself," was qualified by a contradictory "horse-galloping glee" at defeating the King of the Mountain. But the shame he feels for his aunt's humiliation is unqualified and unavoidable. Playing an Oedipal role as a twenty-two-year-old, Milkman acted by instinct more than commitment when he usurped his father's authority. His sister Lena accurately tells him he did not do it so much to protect Ruth as to announce that he was "taking over, letting us know you had the right to tell her and all of us what to do" (216). That "fall" ended in no victory, however, because Milkman rejected the knowledge that it revealed and shirked responsibility for his freedom. In short, he willed to remain in the garden and become his father's lackey. Injuring Pilate, he falls a second time, but this time he heads east of Macon's fallow kingdom. In seeking a future of freedom, he unwittingly discovers a redemptive past and a true community.

In the mythical journey to Pennsylvania and Virginia, Milkman reaches various levels of knowledge, learning at first about the history of the Deads and ultimately about himself. The "flight" transforms a search for gold into a search for a past—and consequently a meaningful present. When Reverend Cooper recounts the story of his family, Milkman feels "a glow" (231). And the more the old men in town recall "Lincoln's Heaven," his grandfather's farm, "the more he [misses] something in his life" (234). He finds out about his father and aunt's near-Edenic past, which even Macon cannot talk about without his voice turning "less hard" (52). The farm nestled against the "prettiest mountain you ever saw," bore fruit trees and housed animals in its woods before it was turned into dairy land by the white Butler family who stole it. Pilate, called a "wild-wood girl" when she was growing up, maintains the association with nature in her pine-scented shack, which is filled with the odor of fermenting fruit. That is why Milkman felt "completely happy" there from the beginning and why Macon stole to the window one night, "softening under the weight of memory and music" (30). Pilate's "notorious winehouse" is the closest thing to "home" in the city. In contrast to the selfish avarice dominant in Macon's white kingdom, Lincoln's Heaven reflects community. Susan Blake aptly notes that whereas Macon's father, Jake, succeeded in affirming community "at the expense of the white folks" he outsmarted, Macon achieves "success at the expense of black folks."[8] Having grown up in his father's inverted Eden, Milkman finds in Pennsylvania the paradise of a lost innocence.

Though as a child Milkman could not recognize the boy his father reminisced about in "that stern, greedy, unloving man," he now "[loves] the boy and [loves] that boy's father" (234–35). Milkman can see that Macon "had an

8. "Folklore and Community in *Song of Solomon*," *MELUS* 7, no. 3 (1980): 81-82.

intimate relationship" with his own father, who "loved him, trusted him, and found him worthy of working 'right alongside' him" (234). Milkman envisions his father in lost innocence; he glimpses his father's worthiness as "Old Macon Dead's boy" (236). It is significant, therefore, that the ancient Circe confuses Milkman with his father when Milkman meets her in the rotting Butler estate: "I knew one day you would come back" (240). Symbolically, Milkman recovers his father's past and secures the opportunity to gain the spiritual wholeness his father lost when he first tried to take the white man's gold.

Locating the remarkable Circe at the Butler estate by traveling through a symbolic birth canal, "a greenish black tunnel" (238), Milkman pieces more of his history together. The profoundly mythic Circe speaks like a "twenty-year-old girl" (240) and sexually arouses Milkman despite her one-hundred-plus years. In her total desecration of the Butlers, she signals Milkman's own victory over the white man's material greed and the values venerated by the already-lost Macon Dead. She sends Milkman to retrace the past by going to the womblike cave where Milkman hoped to find the gold and where Jake Dead's remains had been placed when they floated up from the shallow grave Macon had dug near the river. He undergoes rites of passage: an underground journey in the cave, a total immersion in water, a tearing of his clothes, a meal of bitter leaves. In direct contrast to the "tended woods" in City Park on Honoré Island, "where tiny convenient paths [lead] you through" (250), these woods restore a lost association with the mythic "wild-woods" identified with Pilate and the hunting ground at Shalimar, Virginia.

But the journey cannot end until Milkman confronts his whole self in his "original home" at Shalimar. In his first visit he plays the haughty urban black, insensitively flaunts his money, and fails to ask anyone's name or to give his own. Easily drawn into a fight by a local black, Saul, he blames the "black Neanderthals" for their treatment and "would have slaughtered everybody in sight"

(269) if he had possessed a weapon. He thinks he has come "home," but finds himself a stranger in paradise, "unknown, unloved, and damned near killed" (270). In fact, the fight marks the first stage in rites of humiliation necessary to gain self-knowledge. He has to fall, to lose his false identity in order to be resurrected from the dead. At first he wonders what the "Neanderthals" are going to do to him, and he aptly puns again on his name: "My name's Macon; I'm already dead."

A mythical night hunt arranged by the older men of the village symbolizes the death of the counterfeit life that Milkman himself recognizes he has been living in the white urban culture. When the men take him into the dark, primal woods, Milkman runs the risk of self-knowledge, stripped of all the resources that have sustained him. "There was nothing here to help him—not his money, his car, his father's reputation, his suit, or his shoes" (277). For the first time completely dependent on himself "and what he was born with, or had learned to use," he fears his ignorance, his inability "to separate out, of all the things there were to sense, the one that life itself might depend on" (277). He begins thinking about Guitar, who has followed him south, realizing that his brother has been brutalized and bastardized by loss of contact with the restorative powers associated with nature. Ironically, even as the surface roots of a gum tree cradle Milkman "like the rough but maternal hands of a grandfather," Guitar tries to strangle him with a wire.

Later, after Milkman is saved from Guitar by shooting off his gun and attracting the other hunters, he feels "exhilarated by simply walking the earth . . . his legs [are] stalks, tree trunks. . . . And he [does] not limp" (281). He begins to embody the ancient ancestor Macon knew existed somewhere in history, "some lithe young man with onyx legs as straight as cane stalks" (17). And his consciousness expands when he watches the men eviscerate the bobcat. As the body is skinned and stripped, Milkman recalls Guitar's warning words to him that "Everybody wants a black man's life. Not his dead life; I mean his living life." As Dorothy Lee has observed, in each act of dismemberment "Milkman sees that, for Guitar, the blackman's 'condition' is defined by the flaying and evisceration of the cat." She goes on,

> The flesh slit by the hunters could be Guitar's or his victims' or both. He is, after all, externalizing his own 'murder' in killing others. . . . It is clear too that the hunters love the beast they dissect. The hunt is about love—Guitar and Milkman, the men and the cat, the participants and the community.

Furthermore, in being offered the heart and instructed to eat it, Milkman takes on the attributes of the bobcat. Lee concludes, "the animal becomes a spiritual father to its killer."[9] In a sense, the scene depicts an exorcism of Guitar's murderous potential in Milkman, who a short time before "would have slaughtered everybody in sight" (269). The cat's death reveals Milkman's understanding of Guitar's demonic power and so his escape from it. But it is also an embracing of his Cain-like brother. Though he has to meet Guitar one last time in the woods, Milkman has "felt a sudden rush of affection" (278) for his Other and the "maimed" and "scarred" blacks who form a common humanity.

The humiliation Milkman suffers on the hunt makes him worthy to receive the knowledge of his past, thereby freeing him from his spurious garden. He freely accepts humiliation. At the cost of his pride, he willingly lies about shooting off the gun: "I dropped the gun; I tripped and it went off. Then when I picked it up it went off again" (280). In ironic truth he admits he was "Scared to death." He proves worthy of staying with Sweet, symbol of the "natural goodness" of Shalimar. For the first time, Milkman gives of himself to a woman: he bathes her, washes her hair, massages her back, makes her bed, washes her dishes, and touches her face. Lena had told him just before he left for Pennsylvania that her and

9. "*Song of Solomon*: To Ride the Air," 69.

58

Corinthian's "girlhood was spent on him" and that he still is "a sad, pitiful, stupid, selfish, hateful man" (218). His abuse of Hagar gives validity to her claim. But having undergone transfiguration on the hunt, Milkman can give as well as take from Shalimar's "nice lady."

His evolving character also earns him access to Susan Byrd, who can provide missing parts of his family history. After his first visit to her house, he watches the children gather to sing in the early morning: "Again their sweet voices [remind] him of the gap in his own childhood" (299). He remembers Pilate when he hears the children and is "homesick for her, for her house, for the very people he had been hell-bent to leave"—Pilate, his mother, even his father. Naked after a fall, he endures the shame of self-consciousness: "Hating his parents, his sisters, seemed silly now. And the skin of shame he had rinsed away in the bathwater after having stolen from Pilate returned. . . . His mind turned to Hagar and how he had treated her at the end. Why did he never sit down and talk to her? Honestly" (300–301).

Chastened, he can now discover the links between Pilate's old blues song, "O Sugarman don't leave me here," the very requiem Pilate sang when Robert Smith was about to jump from the hospital, and the children's song, "Solomon don't leave me here." He is "as excited as a child confronted with boxes and boxes of presents under the skirt of a Christmas tree" (304). After he returns to Susan Byrd's house to fill in the missing pieces of the story, he takes Sweet swimming in the river, ostensibly washing off the dirt, but in truth purging himself of "All that jewelry . . . all that shit," that had weighed him down. His great grandfather Solomon could fly—and so perhaps can he. He can "hardly wait to go home" (329) and tell Pilate and Macon the truth.

When he returns, remorseful for his violation of love and fully aware that "he had never so much as made . . . a cup of tea" for Pilate or Ruth, the two who from the beginning conspired to save his life, he is greeted by Pilate's breaking a bottle over his head for causing Hagar's death. Aware of his own culpability, he recalls Sweet's poignant question about his great grandfather Solomon's flight: "Who'd he leave behind?" (332). Having abandoned Hagar as Solomon abandoned Ryna and his twenty-one children, he knows Hagar's death was "his fault." Later, when Pilate determines to bury a green and white shoe box of Hagar's hair along with her father's bones, Milkman claims the box as token of his remorse. Possessing it, Milkman tries, however feebly, to pay homage to the one he destroyed. Hagar thought he did not like her black-woman's hair, that he loved the "silky hair" and "Penny-colored hair" ("and lemon-colored skin" and "gray-blue eyes") of the black girls on Honoré Island who wanted to be white. But prophetically, Pilate had told her, "He got to love it" because "How can he love himself and hate you hair?" (315). Now able to respect his blackness and racial identity, Milkman takes Hagar's hair as an icon of his black consciousness and his love.

Despite his personal victory, he seems unable to alter his home. Morrison's insistence on realism allows no simplistic resolutions. The journey east of Eden can be made only at great risk and with no promise except to the self who ventures out. Pilate and Macon are not reconciled, Milkman's father is not "a bit interested" in Solomon's remarkable flight, the Seven Days will keep looking for a new recruit, Ruth and Macon will continue their sterile relationship, and "the consequence of Milkman's own stupidity would remain, and regret would always outweigh the things he was proud of having done. Hagar was dead and he had not loved her a bit. And Guitar was . . . somewhere" (335).

It matters that Milkman drives rather than flies with Pilate to bury Jake's bones at Solomon's Leap; for, as Milkman will come to know, Pilate knows how to fly "without ever leaving the ground" (336). Freedom can be purchased only by confronting reality, represented by contact with the earth. For Milkman this means an encounter with Guitar. He already realizes he cannot "let him direct and determine" his life or he will "run me off the earth" (294).

Once more in the dark woods Milkman has to "defeat that Shadow," as Marlow has to defeat his shadow, Kurtz, in Conrad's *Heart of Darkness* or as Ed Gentry has to defeat his enemy-brother, the mountaineer, in James Dickey's *Deliverance*. Guitar will try to kill his brother because he thinks Milkman lacks the racial consciousness he demands and because by destroying him he hopes to annihilate that part of himself he most fears, the part that rebels against his cruelty to whites, that challenges his absolutism. He will try to kill Milkman to preserve his innocence, murdering him in order to quiet moral consciousness in himself. Milkman had warned Guitar that his violence was self-destructive and that "If you do it enough, you can do it to anybody" (161). Yet for Milkman to defeat Guitar is also to accommodate him, paradoxically to be saved from his cruel indifference by offering himself to him.

The novel's ending has generated much lively debate. Though most see it as victorious, others question its near sentimentality. Diane Bowman, for example, has wondered if Milkman's "flying" at Guitar "is an escape from self or from others, an escape achieved at the expense of others . . . whatever personal growth his odyssey has affected, Milkman's energy remains invested in himself, his personal 'high.'"[10] And James W. Coleman has complained on nonaesthetic grounds that Pilate and Milkman's "personal" achievements do not "affect or change destructive Black lifestyles."[11] But it is difficult not to see the end as an existential and moral victory, existential because Milkman has at last achieved selfhood, and moral because, unlike Solomon, he has at last assumed responsibility for the community. Joyce M. Wegs offers the interesting reading that Milkman leaps toward Guitar "not necessarily to take his life but perhaps to save through active love the life of the man he still regards as

10. "Flying High: The American Icarus in Morrison, Roth, and Updike," *Perspectives on Contemporary Literature* 8 (1982): 13.
11. "Beyond the Reach of Love and Caring: Black Life in Toni Morrison's *Song of Solomon*," *Obsidian II* 1, no. 3 (1986): 151–61.

'his brother.'" Surely Milkman's relationship with Guitar is not simply that of enemy: "Would you save my life or would you take it? Guitar was exceptional. To both questions he could answer yes" (331). As the ambiguous serpent, Guitar has liberated Milkman from his debilitating garden. But he also threatens to destroy him psychologically and physically. It is worth noting that Milkman does not fly *from* Guitar and that Guitar puts down his rifle. When Milkman "leaps," does he do so to embrace the one who ironically has driven him toward spiritual freedom?[12]

Morrison has said, "I don't shut doors at the end of books. There is always a resolution of a sort but there are always possibilities—choices. . . ."[13] The choice Milkman makes is dictated by his astounding discovery that he loves Pilate because "without even leaving the ground, she could fly" (336), a truth symbolized by a bird flying away with the box-earrings bearing her name. The only "flight" possible to Milkman is also symbolic, a spiritual and psychological flight assured when he no longer evades but offers himself to his brother: "'You want my life? . . . You need it? Here'" (337). Here is true freedom from self-bondage in a spurious garden, a fortunate fall that is as well an act of flight.

12. "Toni Morrison's *Song of Solomon*: A Blues Song," *Essays in Literature* 9, no. 2 (1982): 222.

13. Bessie W. Jones, "An Interview with Toni Morrison," in Bessie W. Jones and Audrey L. Vinson, *The World of Toni Morrison* (Dubuque, Iowa: Kendall/Hunt, 1985), 135.

TAR BABY

ALTHOUGH the fall pattern informs all the novels discussed, *Tar Baby* employs it more explicitly than any other narrative. The novel opens in a quintessential paradise, the lush Caribbean estate where a retired Philadelphia candy manufacturer, Valerian Street, lives with his much younger wife, Margaret, and his longtime black servants, Sydney and Ondine. Visiting is Jadine, Sydney and Ondine's beautiful niece, whom they have raised. A fashionable Paris model, she has been educated at the Sorbonne with Valerian's money and has spent most of her time in Paris and New York among aesthetes and the wealthy, including a rich European who wants to marry her. The lush setting initiates the fall motif, for as Keith Byerman concludes, "Isle de Chevaliers is a perverse Eden,"[1] an exotic example of the flawed "garden" we have discussed in other works. In a departure from her earlier novels, Morrison seriously treats white characters in *Tar Baby* by incorporating Valerian and Margaret Street in an extensive adaptation of the fall myth. Ultimately, though, the focus falls on the young black couple, Jadine Childs and Son Green, who attempt to flee the physical and spiritual bondage of a white man's garden.

Though the picturesque setting portrays "a remoteness and beauty analogous to the Garden of Eden," as Bessie W. Jones observes, "through this near paradise there are reminders of the Fall," evidence that white society is destroying "the natural beauty and uprooting fowl and animals from their natural habitat."[2] The small community of

1. *Fingering the Jagged Grain: Tradition and Form in Recent Black Fiction* (Athens: University of Georgia Press, 1985), 208.
2. "Garden Metaphor and Christian Symbolism in *Tar Baby*," in Bessie W. Jones and Audrey L. Vinson, *The World of Toni Morrison* (Dubuque, Iowa: Kendall/Hunt, 1985), 116–17. Jones parallels the description of place with Milton's account of Eden after Eve eats the forbidden fruit.

expensive homes had been built by Haitian laborers and constructed above a swamp called Sein de Veilles (witch's tit) that was formed when the white invaders rerouted the river and displaced it to end twenty leagues from the sea. "The world was altered" by wealthy whites: "The men had gnawed the daisy trees until . . . they broke in two and hit the ground. In the huge silence that followed their fall, orchids spiraled down to join them."³ Though seemingly idyllic, the land is rotting, and haunted by demonic forces. The locals tell a story of one hundred blind, black horsemen, descendants of slaves who swam from a sinking French slave ship carrying horses. Their free progeny believe they still ride horses over the dark hills: "They learned to ride through the rain forests avoiding all sorts of trees and things. . . . They race each other, and for sport they sleep with the swamp women on Sein de Veilles" (152–53).

On the edge of this mysterious realm, the white god Valerian Street putters in his greenhouse where he listens to classical music and reads plant catalogues, trying to evade the "disorder and meaninglessness" of the modern world and the sad failure of his own life. The greenhouse represents retreat from the truth of his lost innocence; it is a sanitized world where he can artificially grow the hydrangea that symbolize his innocence and can "talk to his ghosts in peace." More than a retreat, it represents "Valerian's attempt to recapture something that he has lost," to recreate in the greenhouse "the prelapsarian state found in the Edenic setting of man's first paradise."⁴ Yet even after three years of residence, L'Arbe de la Croix, built on the ruins of a once idyllic land, possesses a "tentativeness" and has "a hotel feel about it" (at one point Valerian refers to himself as "the owner and operator of this hotel" [19]). It is another specious garden.

Here, Morrison has remarked, characters do not have

3. *Tar Baby* (New York: Alfred A. Knopf, 1981), 10. Page numbers hereafter in parentheses in the text.
4. Jones, "Garden Metaphor and Christian Symbolism in *Tar Baby*," 119.

the "escape routes that people have in a large city . . . no police to call . . . no close neighbors to interfere." Here, she goes on to say, the characters are "all together in a pressure cooker . . . a kind of Eden."[5] Those living in the paradise, black or white, bring with them evidence of their flawed humanity. They await the serpent who somehow can force them to confront themselves, can make them see the truth that could set them free from their spiritual incapacity.

Enter Son. Like Guitar Bains or Sula, he threatens the tenuous peace and harmony of an already flawed world. The serpent in paradise is a distinctly black outlaw, a fugitive who, similar to Leggett in Conrad's "The Secret Sharer," first appears at night, emerging from the waters of the unconscious self. As a mysterious force reborn into the world, Son swims to the Seabird II (where Jadine and Margaret first appear), previously having been caught in "a wide, empty tunnel" and having ritualistically "turned three times" in the dark water (4). After hiding out in the ship, Son follows the road where the jeep takes Jadine and Margaret to the house. He secretly enters the house, partly from hunger, partly because it looks "cool and civilized" (134). A stranger in paradise, he ventures upstairs "out of curiosity," and is enraptured by the sleeping Jadine, a symbol of refinement and civilization. The house becomes his "nighttime possession" (138), in which he roams as a shadow figure of each character's undiscovered self.

More than the conventional tempter in the garden, Son is the manifestation of the black pariah in Western culture, the terrorizing black male, the supposed rapist of white women. To Margaret and the whitewashed blacks at the estate, he represents the "swamp nigger," a black "beast" who jeopardizes a distinctly white Eden. He is the rebellious black who will not behave according to the rules or values of the system, and it is precisely on such

5. Nellie McKay, "An Interview with Toni Morrison," *Contemporary Literature* 24, no. 4 (1983): 417.

grounds that all the characters except Valerian Street judge him.

It is no small irony that Valerian feels "disappointment nudging contempt for the outrage Jade and Sydney and Ondine exhibit in defending property and personnel that did not belong to them from a black man who was one of their own" (145). The morning after Son's appearance, Valerian recalls his son Michael derisively using the word "bourgeois." Valerian thought it meant "unexciting" until the others condemned Son, and then "he thought [it] meant Uncle Tom-ish" (144). With a touch of whimsy, Valerian compares Son with Michael, who always promises to visit but never does for reasons that surface later. As some critics have noted, Son becomes something of a parody of the Christ figure, a man who, Bessie W. Jones points out, is wrapped in "a fine pair of silk pajamas" in place of "swaddling clothes," put in the "manger" of the guest room, and welcomed as the white god's surrogate only son.[6] We might add that when Son first arrives he notices "the sky holy with stars" (134) and that "here he [is] with the immediate plans of a new born baby" (138). Like the suffering Christ figure who brings redemption, Son is rejected by those he possesses the power to transform.

Indeed, the arrival of the "criminal" in the garden sends the characters scurrying to protect their innocence. Sydney, who prides himself on being "a Phil-a-delphia Negro" (163), wants to call the police and get the "swamp nigger" out as soon as possible. And Ondine, too, rejects him: "The man upstairs wasn't a Negro—meaning one of them. He is a stranger," "a nasty and ignorant . . . nigger" (102). And Jadine is indignant at Margaret's question, "You don't know him do you?" She protests, "Know him? How would I know him?" (128). She had not seen a "black like him" for some ten years, not since she lived on Morgan Street in Baltimore before her mother died and she went to Philadelphia at age twelve to live with her Uncle Sydney and Aunt Ondine. Her subsequent prostitution of her

6. "Garden Metaphor and Christian Symbolism in *Tar Baby*," 115–24.

blackness is illustrated in her "seduction" by the expensive fur coat sent her by her European lover, Ryk. Just before Son enters her room the morning after he is discovered in Margaret's closet, Jadine "lay spread-eagle on the fur, nestling herself into it. It made her tremble. She opened her lips and licked the fur. It made her tremble more. Ondine was right; there was something a little fearful about the coat. No, not fearful, seductive" (112). And later Son suggestively defines her false identity by tracing her pictures in a fashion magazine with his finger as she talks about the expensive jewelry and earrings she is wearing in the layout. She assumes he is going to rape her, but he returns, "Rape? Why do you little white girls think somebody's trying to rape you?" Condemned as white, Jadine feebly responds, "White . . . I am not . . . you know I'm not white" (121), but Son captures her in a truth. It is no wonder she fears him.

Jadine considers Son's hair symbolic of criminality: "Wild, aggressive, vicious hair that needed to be put in jail. Uncivilized, reform school hair. Mau, Mau, Attica, chain-gang hair" (113). Yet she finds in him that part of herself she has long denied. When he grabs her from behind and presses against her, she has to acknowledge her own culpability. "He had jangled something in her that was so repulsive, so awful, and he had managed to make her feel that the thing that repelled her was not in him but in her. That was why she was ashamed" (123). She had sworn at age twelve that she would "never" let herself be victimized by a man mounting her like a dog in heat, yet she cannot deny that Son was drawn to her by her own animal nature, "which she couldn't help but which was her fault just the same" (124). It is not the criminality of desire but self-denial that he exposes. In short Son enters paradise like the biblical serpent, articulates Jadine's forbidden desires, muted by her counterfeit identity, and galvanizes her into action. In his insistence that she acknowledge the "darker" side of herself, the authentic black self obscured in the distorted mirror of her adopted Eden, Son forces Jadine to see the "beast" in the glass.

Until now, conditioned by her sophisticated European education, Jadine is detached from her own blackness, much like Helene Wright or Geraldine or Macon Dead. Eight years earlier when she last saw Michael while on vacation with the Streets, he had accused her of abandoning her people. Though she knew his idealistic scheme of generating social reform by having black welfare mothers "do crafts, pottery, clothing in their homes" was silly, she admitted that he "did make me want to apologize for what I was doing, what I felt. For liking 'Ave Maria' better than gospel music" (74). Yet when they talk about Michael's hopeless plot, Jadine tells Valerian, "Picasso *is* better than an Itumba mask" (74), and she confesses her embarrassment at attending "ludicrous" art shows put on by pretentious blacks in Europe. Michael had encouraged her to return to Morgan Street with Sydney and Ondine to do handicraft. "Can you believe it?" she asks Valerian. "He might have convinced me if we'd had that talk on Morgan Street. But in Orange County on a hundred and twenty acres of green velvet?" (75). She had long since moved into a white society where "the black people she knew wanted what she wanted" and where success required her "only to be stunning. . . . Say the obvious, ask stupid questions, laugh with abandon, look interested, and light up at any display of their humanity if they showed it" (126–27). She simply tells Son, "I belong here. You, motherfucker, do not . . ." (125).

Nonetheless, Son's presence restores something of her black awareness, just as Guitar Bains awakens Milkman's black consciousness in *Song of Solomon*. He prompts her to recall the guilt she felt two months before when a beautiful African woman in a canary yellow dress spit on her in disgust in a Paris street. The manifestation of Jadine's own black heritage, the woman floated through glass like a vision out of her self, an alter ego passing judgment.[7] As

7. Morrison identifies the African woman as "the original self—the self we betray when we lie, the one that is always there. And whatever that self looks like . . . one measures one's self against it" (McKay, "An Interview with Toni Morrison," 422). See also Gloria Nalor and Toni Morrison, "A Conversation," *Southern Review* 21, no. 3 (1985): 572.

with the woman, Jadine is ambivalent toward Son even from the beginning. Her "neck prickled" when she heard Margaret call him a gorilla, even though she herself "had volunteered nigger" (129). And she experienced a "curious embarrassment" as she pictured herself watching "red-necked gendarmes zoom him away in a boat" (126). Somehow Son spoke from her dream consciousness just as the African woman invaded her psyche. The very morning Son was found in the house, Jadine had stared out her window trying to visualize the one hundred black horsemen who supposedly roamed the hills. She had run away from Paris, in part chased by the African woman in yellow who made her feel somehow "inauthentic." On the edge of a fall, Jadine also awaits the tempter who can penetrate her illusory garden, which Son himself describes as "fragile—like a dollhouse for an adult doll" (131).

Son, too, is ambiguous. Though he "burrowed in his plate like an animal" and sat "grunting in monosyllables," sipping from his saucer and wiping up salad dressing with his bread, he is no wild boar. Even Ondine confesses that "he's been here long enough and quiet enough to rape, kill and steal—do whatever he wanted and all he did was eat" (99). Enthralled by Jadine, he had stared at her through the night with an "appetite for her so gargantuan it lost its focus and spread to his eyes, the orange of his shirt, the curtains, the moonlight" (138), but he never violated her, standing before her image like Beast trembling outside Beauty's door in Jean Cocteau's brilliant surrealistic film. When Valerian welcomes him into the civilized circle, he willfully adapts. He puts on a Hickey Freeman suit, apologizes to Jadine and Ondine, begins using "ma'am," "Mr.," and "Sir," and talks about his own "mama" with Ondine. He even tells Valerian how to get rid of ants by using mirrors and revitalizes Valerian's cyclamens by flicking them with his fingers. Valerian accepts Son as surrogate to Michael, the legitimate "son" having turned prodigal, the outlaw "Son" having returned in the guise of the black Other. In so characterizing Son, Morrison makes him something more than "the official heroic black male"[8] some critics see when they read *Tar Baby* as a stereotypical black novel. Criminal and hero, Son projects the ambivalence of the serpent figure—forbidden but unconsciously willed, possessing healing powers but potentially destructive.

Son recalls growing up with Cheyenne, a demon-like lover who always waited outside Mrs. Tylor's house where he took piano lessons. Toward the end of the novel, he tells Jadine how at eighteen he went to Vietnam, was busted, went back to Eloe, Florida, where he grew up, and married the promiscuous but nonetheless innocent Cheyenne. When he came home drunk after a fistfight and found her sleeping with a thirteen-year-old, he ran his car through the house and started a fire that killed her. But like Conrad's ambiguous Leggatt, Son ran away not in simple fear but because, he recalls, "I didn't want their punishment, I wanted my own" (172). Without roots, "sought for but not after," he had spent eight years among Huck Finns, Nigger Jims, Calibans—a Cain "driven across the face of the earth." He also possesses the moral consciousness of a romantic rebel, the ambiguity of the satanic figure in Blake or Melville.

Jadine also responds to him ambivalently. On one hand, she wants to clean, tame, and control him by making him suitable for her cultured white world. When he begins to show his civilized nature, she finds it impossible to resist him. Yet it is his raw, powerful being that most attracts her. At one point he tells Jadine that "there is something in you to be smelled which I have discovered myself. And no seal-skin coat or million-dollar earrings can disguise it" (125). Once when Jadine waits for him to return with gas for the jeep, she gets trapped accidentally in the swamp quicksand of Sein de Veilles. Like Milkman caught in the Virginia woods in *Song of Solomon*, she is stripped of every vestige of civilization, and the "swamp women," who supposedly mate with the

8. Webster Schott, "Toni Morrison: Tearing the Social Fabric," *The Washington Post Book World*, 22 March 1981, 1.

70

legendary black horsemen, temporarily claim her. Suggestively, though, it is not until the ill-fated Christmas dinner that Jadine and the other characters confront the devastating self-knowledge that drives them out of paradise.

Here all the lies concocted to preserve innocence prove futile. For long years Margaret and Valerian had evaded the truth, Sydney and Ondine had settled into a passive acquiescence, and Jadine had sacrificed her blackness to succeed in white society. As they approach Christmas day, their lives have been suddenly regenerated by Son's coming. New hope arises: Valerian and Margaret sleep together for the first time in many years, Jadine awakens from long self-repression, there is renewed hope that Michael really will come, and even Valerian's plants begin to thrive under Son's "black magic." Again like a Christ, Son seemingly "made something grow that was dying." Yet when Valerian fires the black servants Gideon and Thérèse because they were stealing apples, paradise falls. It is fitting that Thérèse takes the apples because they represent knowledge in this fraudulent Eden. Dorothy Lee interprets the apples as "the fertilizing knowledge of the folk, the insight of the blind Thérèse as opposed to the material and worldly values."[9] For Thérèse, above all others, condemns the Uncle Tom blacks at L'Arbe de la Croix: "machete-hair" Ondine, "bow tie" Sydney, and the "bitch" Jadine.

Son's illusion that Valerian is a worthy white man collapses, and he sees in the rich man's harsh gesture the suppression he had found in other white oppressors— "this one here would chew a morsel of ham and drink secure in the knowledge that he had defecated on two people who had dared to want some of his apples" (204). Representative of the system, Valerian, Son now surmises, "probably thought he was a law-abiding man, they

9. "The Quest for Self: Triumph and Failure in the Works of Toni Morrison," *Black Women Writers (1950–1980): A Critical Evaluation*, ed. Mari Evans (Garden City, N.Y.: Anchor Press/Doubleday, 1984), 357.

all did, and they all always did . . . but they could defecate over a whole people and come there to live and defecate some more by tearing up the land . . ." (203). Valerian could see in Son's eyes "one hundred black men on one hundred unshod horses" (206). The precarious balance of deceit that had sustained the garden can no longer be endured—the truth gives witness to a fallen world.

All stand exposed. The community of whites and blacks, owners and servants, is torn asunder when Son, the outcast, threatens the order. His rebellion against Gideon and Thérèse's dismissal reveals the lies each character has grasped to guard against self-knowledge. His anger releases Ondine's long held secret. In her violent outcry she confesses that Margaret had abused Michael as a child. As a nineteen-year-old mother, Margaret, once "the Principal Beauty of Maine," had stuck pins into Michael and burned him with cigarettes. She had grown up satisfied in a "tacky" trailer in South Suzanne until, at fourteen, she became conscious of her beauty and so lost her innocence. Married by the insistent Valerian when she was only seventeen, Margaret moved into his wealthy home, where she felt the intimidating presence of Valerian's ex-wife and "stiffened like Joan Fontaine in *Rebecca*," fearful of "the pearl-gray *S* on the sheet hems and pillow slips coiled at her" (58). Driven to perversion by a profound loneliness, she had tortured her son. Still wanting desperately to believe that Michael loved her and would return for her sake at Christmas, she had tried to recreate the trailer she grew up in in her bedroom at L'Arbe de la Croix, a futile attempt to recover innocence, like Jadine's "dollhouse" room and Valerian's greenhouse. Then the "nigger in the woodpile," the serpent haunting her unconscious, invaded her reconstructed paradise. Ondine had forewarned that Margaret had "a lot of cleaning up to do with Michael. It's sitting on her heart and she's never going to have no peace until she cleans it up" (192). The revelation of her guilt at last allows Margaret to dream "the dream she ought to have had. . . . The wonderful relief of public humiliation, the solid security of the pillory, were upon her" (235). Finally, she "felt clean, weightless" without the awful burden of innocence. Paradoxically, she is made morally alive.

But the guilt is a composite guilt in which Valerian also shares. He too yearns to go to Michael, "Find him, touch him, rub him, hold him in his arms" (232), but he himself had caused Margaret's loneliness, had driven her to see her child as a threat to her in "its prodigious appetite for security," in its "criminal arrogance" (236). Ondine rightly tells Jadine that Margaret "didn't stick pins in her baby. She stuck em in his baby. Her baby she loved" (279). Responding to her profound if reassuring guilt, Margaret seeks a reconciling punishment from Valerian, asking him to hit her. He always responds, "Tomorrow, perhaps, tomorrow," because he is too incapacitated by his own guilt to strike Margaret. While she seeks absolution by washing her red hair again and again and drying it in the sun "against every instruction ever given her about the care of her hair" (235), Valerian isolates himself in his greenhouse. Shattered by self-knowledge, he knows his culpability: "He thought about innocence there in his greenhouse and knew that he was guilty of it because he had lived with a woman who made something kneel down in him the first time he saw her, but about whom he knew nothing." He "had watched his son grow and talk but also about him he had known nothing." He had found his two-year-old son hiding and singing under the sink, but he chose not to know the truth. Choosing not to know, he "was guilty of innocence," and there was "something in the crime of innocence so revolting it paralyzed him. He had not known because he had not taken the trouble to know" (242).

Though Morrison gives Valerian a measure of sympathy as he remembers losing his own childhood the day a black, toothless washerwoman told him his father was dead, she speaks decidedly of his guilt in one of her most eloquent passages: "An innocent man is a sin before God. Inhuman and therefore unworthy. No man should live without absorbing the sins of his kind, the foul air of his innocence, even if it did wilt rows of angel trumpets and cause them to fall from their vines" (243). Pearl Bell's contention that Morrison's own feelings toward Valerian vacillate between "fondness and outrage"[10] may in fact be true, but the outrage is directed to more than his racism, and the "fondness" exceeds mere sentimentality. His ambiguous nature, worthy both of judgment and compassion, results from his essential flawed humanity, not simply from his whiteness.

Even Ondine and Sydney share in the crime. Ondine had not stopped Margaret from torturing Michael even though she witnessed her cruelty. When Ondine protests that she did not stop Margaret because it was not her job, Margaret responds, "No, it's not your job, Ondine. But I wish it had been your duty, I wish you had liked me enough to help me" (241). Margaret exposes the same capacity for criminal innocence in Ondine that Valerian discovers in himself: ". . . you felt good hating me, didn't you? I could be the mean white lady and you could be the good colored one" (240). By not challenging Margaret's actions, Ondine assumed ownership of the crime: "But once I started keeping it—then it was like my secret too" (241). But knowledge always devastates innocence. Whereas before the dinner "everything was all right, the best it could be and exactly the way she had hoped it would be" in her "own territory where she alone governed" (96), Ondine also watches her Eden collapse under the weight of truth.

Even before the fateful dinner, Sydney knew already in his dreams that he lived in a false paradise with Valerian Street. He prided himself on being "one of those Philadelphia Negroes," but each night he dreamed his "tiny dream" of the lost Eden in Baltimore that he gave up for security and position. Even after over fifty years, "his most vivid dreams were the red rusty Baltimore of 1921. The fish, the trees, the music, the horses' harnesses.

10. "Self-Seekers," *Commentary*, August 1981, 57.

It was a tiny dream he . . . would never recollect from morning to morning. So he never knew what it was exactly that refreshed him" (61). Having become a Philadelphia Negro, he lived in servitude to a white god whose values he parroted until truth destroyed his comfortable world. Margaret told Valerian with too much truth that "Kingfish and Beulah" will always stay: "They are yours for life" (31). It is no small irony that at the end of the novel Sydney assumes control of L'Arbe de la Croix and its failing god.

After the fall Valerian and Margaret seem to be beyond recovery, and Sydney and Ondine appear fated to remain with Valerian and Margaret. Only Son and Jadine act. They leave the irreparable garden to go to New York, where Jadine intends to assimilate Son into her high society world. The contraries cannot coexist, though, and neither character proves capable of integrating the opposite. Gideon had warned Son about Jadine: "Your first yella? . . . look out. It's hard for them not to be white. Hard, I'm telling you. Most never make it" (155).[11] Jadine's acceptance of white values is reflected in her urban environment. She is pure city—Baltimore, Philadelphia, Paris, New York. And Son is all rural Florida—"Eloe." He stands outside the white system, a riotous Cain; she sells herself to the moneyed urban culture. Yet, fleeing the debunked Edenic island, they try vainly to stay together. In contrast to Jadine's easy indifference, Son cannot help empathizing with the outcast blacks he finds in the city. Once, while working a demeaning job loading boxes, he brings home a wild, tempestuous black woman who reminds him of his sister. A direct contrast to Jadine, she is cursing a man in the middle of traffic, shouting obscenities in "the voice of a sergeant," her "face . . . as tight and mean as

11. Trudier Harris argues that Son is attracted to Jadine because he has "an irresistible passion for the white goddess" and that Jadine as "the tar baby becomes the white woman who lures black men into affection for them, but who can never return that affection" (*Exorcising Blackness: Historical and Literary Lynching and Burning Rituals* [Bloomington: Indiana University Press, 1984], 159–62).

broccoli" (227), her eyes narrow and angry, a ring glittering in her nose. Embracing this seemingly unlovable primal being, Son takes her to dinner with Jadine and then back to their apartment, where she steals his change and leaves during the night. Although within Jadine's world, Son cannot be of it.

For her part, Jadine temporarily finds something restorative in Son's impulsiveness and powerful black pride. "He unorphaned her completely. Gave her a brand-new childhood" (229). But clearly Son cannot live comfortably in Jadine's self-constructed paradise, and when Son takes her to his lost Eden in Eloe, it is apparent that she cannot live in his world either. With its apparent poverty and ignorance and isolation, Eloe defines all the "blackness" Jadine has long struggled to escape. To Son it represents the opposite: self-worth, wholeness, and human values. Long separated from his father because he fled after his wife's death, Son carries with him the guilt of a prodigal son. Though he had written money orders to his father, he feels ashamed that he had never written a note. His father had cashed only a few of the checks, in part because Son wrote his name on them, and he treasured Son's handwriting: "Pretty. Like your mama" (250). A returned prodigal suffering remorse, Son honors his father's moral judgment that Jadine should not stay in his house if she and Son are not married. Made morally sensitive, Son insists to Jadine that she stay at his Aunt Rosa's modest house.

Jadine, too, becomes morally alive. She experiences profound self-awareness when Aunt Rosa accidentally sees her naked in bed: "No man made her feel that naked, that unclothed. Leerers, lovers, doctors, artists—none of them had made her feel exposed. More than exposed. Obscene" (253). Here too she dreams of judgment. She sees all the black women in her life in the dark outside the door: "The night women were not merely against her . . . not merely looking superior over their sagging breasts and folded stomachs, they seemed somehow in agreement about her, and they were out to get her, tie her, bind

76

her. Grab the person she had worked hard to become and choke it off wih their soft loose tits" (262). More than the conventional metaphysical or psychological ghosts that haunt characters in literature, these are racial ghosts, black women who stand in judgment of Jadine's abandonment of her racial being. Not Dawn, Aisha, Felicite, or Betty ("They were her friends. They were like her." [261]), these are the "night women," who, like Son, demand recognition of her racial consciousness.

Even when he first sees her sleeping at Valerian's estate, Son yearns "to press his dreams" into Jadine's consciousness, to will her out of the white man's house and into a world of "fat black ladies in white dresses minding the pie table in the basement of the church and white wet sheets flapping on the line" (119). Yet he fears that she might "press her dreams of gold and cloisonne and honey-colored silk into him" (120). Though Son devastates Valerian's white paradise, he cannot reclaim her. His failure becomes apparent when Jadine tells him that while he was playing criminal by driving his car into his wife's bed and hiding from the law, she was being educated with the help of a "poor old white dude." "Stop loving your ignorance," she tells him; "it isn't lovable" (264). Nor can he himself deny his failure, his "shame" at not looking into Cheyenne's face as she was dying, at not writing a note to his father, at his "loving his ignorance." He informs Jadine that what they taught her in college "didn't include me" and so they kept her ignorant: "because until you know about me, you don't know nothing about yourself" (264). But he, too, is from the beginning a wanderer in search of self. Morrison concludes, "One had a past, the other a future and each one bore the culture to save the race in his hands. Mama-spoiled black man, will you mature with me? Culture-bearing black woman, whose culture are you bearing?" (269)

Like the conclusion to *Song of Solomon*, the ending of this novel has provoked considerable controversy. Some critics read it as optimistic and affirmative. Bessie W. Jones goes so far as to call it the attainment of a "new Eden, a celestial paradise." On the other hand, James W. Coleman concludes that Morrison pulls "an escape act by imposing on the novel a superficial good ending that, under analysis, proves unsatisfactory." Cynthia Dubin Edelberg complains that in Son's flight Morrison "posits a kind of primitivism as an answer, as something that counters education and work, but this primitivism is rhetorical rather than convincing."[12] Morrison herself has admitted to uncertainty. "I may have some attitude which one is more right than the other [Son or Jadine], but in a funny sense that book was very unsettling to me because everybody was sort of wrong." Yet in the same interview, she relates the novel, as she does her other fiction, to Greek drama and comments, "There was probably . . . catharsis in the sense of a combination of the restoration of order—order is restored at the end—and the character having a glimmer of some knowledge that he didn't have when the book began."[13] Finally, though, the knowledge both characters gain seems to lead to an incomplete catharsis. Neither Jadine nor Son achieves a full victory in defeat.

Coming to a frightening awareness, naked after the fall, Jadine eludes the truth. Like Blake's Thel, who scurries back to the vales of Har, Jadine flees back to the elite society she considers her paradise. Incapable of committing a saving sin against her security, she will never integrate her other self. According to Susan Lydon, Jadine is caught between her sex and her race. To be true to her freedom as a woman, she must resist Son's male insistence that she play the subservient role of "fat black ladies" serving pies in the church basement. To be true to her black heritage, however, she needs to sacrifice success

12. Jones, "Garden Metaphor and Christian Symbolism in *Tar Baby*," 124; Coleman, "The Quest for Wholeness in Toni Morrison's *Tar Baby*," *Black American Literature Forum* 20, nos. 1/2 (1986): 69; Edelberg, "Morrison's Voice: Formal Education, the Work Ethic and the Bible," *American Literature* 58, no. 2 (1986): 236.

13. Bessie W. Jones, "An Interview with Toni Morrison," in Bessie W. Jones and Audrey L. Vinson, *The World of Toni Morrison* (Dubuque, Iowa: Kendall/Hunt, 1985), 135.

in a white culture. Says Lydon, "she is neither female enough nor black enough to make it in her culture."[14] Viewed in this context, Jadine's "fall" leads to no regeneration. Cast east of Eden she exists in unresolved duality, knowing "good" and "evil," black and white.

Nor can Son survive. Looking at the photographs from Eloe after Jadine has left him, he discovers a lost paradise. "It all looked miserable . . . sad, poor and even poor spirited" (295). He cannot go home again. As his father remarks when Son tells him he could have lied about being married to Jadine, "But you didn't lie. You told the truth and you got to live by the truth" (249). When he returns to the island looking frantically for Jadine, the wise Thérèse, descendant of the blind horsemen, asks, "If you cannot find her what will you do? Live in the garden of some other white people house?" (305). She tells him to forget Jadine because "she has forgotten her ancient properties" (305). And finally she offers him the only possible escape—joining the legendary horsemen in the hills. "They are waiting for you. They are naked and they are black too . . . Go there. Choose them" (306). Elizabeth House argues that Son is "the rabbit" that escapes to the briars, "that Jadine, the tar baby, will not successfully lure Son again."[15] Perhaps so, but Morrison allows Son no victory separate from the timeless world of legend and darkness. Becoming an eternal night rider returning to the dark unconscious from which he emerged, Son retreats from a world where he can find no reconciliation and no solution to his own fallen humanity.

Jadine and Son, Valerian and Margaret, Sydney and Ondine, all bear the consequences of self-knowledge. The fall motif in *Tar Baby* makes Morrison's work considerably more substantial and meaningful than some critics have contended. To be sure, Morrison partly follows in the tradition of American literature by depicting the es-

14. "What's an Intelligent Woman To Do?" *The Village Voice*, 1–7 July 1981, 41.

15. "The 'Sweet Life' in Toni Morrison's Fiction," *American Literature* 56, no. 2 (1984): 201.

sential conflict between primitivity and civilization, the rural and the urban—redskin and paleface. But beyond this conventional dialectic, *Tar Baby,* like her other novels, describes the passage from innocence to experience with biblical and theological overtones—garden images, references to the serpent, expressions of guilt and lost innocence, a yearning to return to the garden.

BELOVED

IN one of the few strongly negative reviews of *Beloved*, Stanley Crouch labels the Pulitzer Prize-winning novel "a blackface holocaust novel . . . written in order to enter American slavery into the big-time of martyr ratings contests." He goes on to accuse Morrison of trying to "placate feminist ideology" while "appropriating the conventions of a holocaust tale." Morrison, he concludes, ignores the "ambiguities of the human soul" and opts for the simplistic portrayal of good and evil.[1]

Hardly. More than any of Morrison's novels, *Beloved* integrates racial history with a discerning revelation of moral ambiguity, racial consciousness with a description of the reciprocal relationship between good and evil and with the paradoxical theme of losing innocence to achieve "higher innocence." *Beloved* is the culmination of Morrison's depiction of the paradoxical nature of good and evil, particularly in its portrayal of the victimization of children. Not even Cholly Breedlove's rape of his daughter or Eva Peace's burning of her son can match in horror Sethe's slitting of her daughter's throat and near smashing of her newborn child. Yet, like Cholly and Eva, Sethe acts out of a profound and unrelenting love.

As in the earlier novels, however much Morrison describes the reality of white cruelty and the pervasive ability of a depraved system to corrupt the oppressed as well as the oppressor, she also insists in *Beloved* on the necessity of personal responsibility. Her latest novel describes evil as all-encompassing, evident not just in the overt sadism of many Southern whites (which is, after all, a fact of history) but also in the "banality of evil," to use Hannah Arendt's phrase, in the "nice Nazi" nature of the kindly slave-owners the Garners and even more in the

---

1. "Aunt Medea," *The New Republic*, 19 October 1987, 38–43.

potential for evil within the black community itself. Evil persists in the "meanness" of the blacks who refuse to warn Sethe about the white men come to reclaim her, in the well-intended Stamp Paid's betrayal of Sethe's past, in Paul D's cowardly retreat, and most profoundly, in Sethe's criminal love itself. Far from asking readers only to "tally up the sins committed against the darker race and feel sorry for them," as Crouch contends, Morrison asks us to enter the consciousness of a woman not just brutalized by the savagery of an evil institution but haunted by her own capacity for violence against the very object of her love. Contrary to what Crouch implies, Sethe must and does pay a price for the criminality of her love—whatever sympathy Morrison asks us to feel for Sethe, she never denies the awful truculence of her deed. It is understandable but not excusable. And until Beloved returns to demand an accounting, a reconciliation with the past, Sethe lacks the self-knowledge necessary to her freedom.

There is no question, of course, that slavery and its proponents are the consummate evil in the novel and that this gives the work a polemical bias. But Morrison has never denied the political nature of her work and, in fact, has argued that the "political" dimension of literature is essential to its value:

The work must be political. It must have that as its thrust. That's a pejorative term in critical circles now: if a work of art has any political influence in it, somehow it's tainted. My feeling is just the opposite: if it has none it is tainted. . . . The best art is political and you ought to be able to make it unquestionably political and irrevocably beautiful at the same time.[2]

The moral authority of Beloved resides less in a revelation of the obvious horrors of slavery than in a revelation of slavery's nefarious ability to invert moral categories and

2. "Rootedness: The Ancestor as Foundation," in Black Women Writers (1950–1980): A Critical Evaluation, ed. Mari Evans (Garden City, N.Y.: Anchor Press/Doubleday, 1984), 344–45.

behavior and to impose tragic choice. Like a Greek protagonist faced with a tragic dilemma, Sethe opts to kill Beloved because, paradoxically, "if I hadn't killed her she would have died."[3] Unable to avert choice, Sethe sacrifices her innocence, and even if it is "the only thing to do," Morrison grants her no reprieve from judgment. Far from the melodramatic "Aunt Medea" Crouch tries to make her, Sethe is driven by unbounded love for "the best part" of herself. Yet Morrison no more exonerates Sethe from responsibility for her action than Sophocles excuses Oedipus. Her deed carries the paradoxical qualities of an existential victory and a moral offense. One fact is certain: Sethe, unlike Medea, cannot evade the consequences of choice. There is a price to be paid. "To Sethe the future was a matter of keeping the past at bay" (42), Morrison tells us, but it is memory that enslaves her present. However much the abhorrence of slavery makes *Kindermord* "the right thing to do," Morrison has remarked that "she had no right to do it."[4] Guilty in Kafka's memorable phrase "irrespective of crime," Sethe, like the tragic heroine, must confront her past, made incarnate in Beloved.

At first a poltergeist harassing 124 Bluestone, "an evil thing looking for more" (37), according to the community, Beloved assumes flesh after Paul D chases her vengeful spirit from the house. When he asks Denver toward the end of the novel if she thought Beloved was really her sister come from the grave, Denver replies, "At times. At times I think she was—more" (266). Clearly she is a composite symbol, not just Sethe's dead child come to exact judgment, but also the representative of the "Sixty Million and More" to whom Morrison alludes in her headnote: "The best educated guess at the number of black Africans who never made it into slavery—those who died either as captives in Africa or on the slave ships."[5] The marks

3. *Beloved* (New York: Alfred A. Knopf, 1987), 200. Page numbers hereafter in parentheses in the text.

4. Interview, "MacNeil-Lehrer Newshour," PBS, 29 September 1987.

5. Walter Clemons, "The Ghosts of 'Sixty Million More,'" *Newsweek*, 28 November 1987, 75.

identifying her as Sethe's murdered child, the three scratches on her forehead where Sethe held her steady while she slit her throat, were "so fine and thin they seemed first like hair, baby hair before it bloomed and roped into the masses of black yarn under her hat" (51). Though the stranger is no longer a child but the twenty-year-old she would have been had she lived, Beloved assumes the person of a newborn. She has "new skin" and "soft and new" hands and feet, and she emerges from the water. When Sethe first sees her and her bladder fills to capacity so quickly she cannot make it to the privy, she recalls "flooding the boat when Denver was born" (51), as though reenacting the birth ritual.

But Morrison incorporates "something more." Water serves not only to symbolize rebirth but the torturous passage of a slave ship en route to America. In the brief passage where Morrison permits Beloved to articulate her "unspeakable thoughts," Beloved relates her flight from "the other side" to escape from a slave ship—her lungs "hurt most of all" (50). She evokes life on the overcrowded boat where she is forced to crouch in the ship's belly with a dead man's face pressed against her, where "men without skin bring their morning water to drink we have none," where "the iron circle is around our neck" (210–13). She tells Denver that she was hot "over there." "Nothing to breathe down there and no room to move in" (75)—the ship as grave. Beloved, then, "is both Sethe's doomed infant and one of the "Sixty Million and More," a victim both of Sethe's "rough love" and the manifest cruelty of slavers.

What is more, she becomes a demonic force returned to punish and to redeem Sethe, a remarkably ambiguous force able to "free" Sethe at last from her past, but only by exacting an enormous price; she is on one hand "an evil thing," on the other a Christ figure come to save. At one point Ella says of the ghost at 124 that "people who die bad don't stay in the ground," and Stamp Paid must agree: "I couldn't deny it. Jesus Christ himself didn't" (188). When she fears Beloved has left her forever after suddenly disappearing from the woodshed, Denver grabs the hem of her murdered sister's garment like the suppliant touching Christ's robe: "I thought you left me. I thought you went back" (123). Beloved is the spirit made flesh, the "beloved" one come to reclaim Sethe and from whom Sethe seeks forgiveness. But she is also "full of spite" and destructive energy like Sula and Guitar. Her ambivalence is nowhere more apparent than in the scene in the Clearing when she seemingly usurps the place of Baby Suggs' spirit, which is gently stroking Sethe's throat, and begins choking her mother. When Denver accuses her, Beloved denies it: "I kissed her neck. I didn't choke it. The circle of iron choked it" (101). In this complex scene Morrison exposes Beloved's dual nature, revealing her ruthless power and her ability to free Sethe from the "circle of iron," the mark of the slavery that drives her from innocence.

Beloved's resurrection coerces Sethe and the others involved to return to and reenact the past, again like tragic figures doomed to reenact it in memory and deed. Looking back, they begin to understand themselves and to reassess where they have been. They now know the ironically named Sweet Home to be the most illusory of Edens. Before Mr. Garner's death and schoolteacher's arrival, it camouflaged the evil enterprise it represented. However kindly the Garners were, they still perpetuated the organized criminality of slavery. When they let Halle buy Baby Suggs' freedom, she, at least, sensed the irony of the Garners' generosity: "But you got my boy and I'm all brokedown. You be renting him out to pay for me way after I'm gone to Glory" (146). Although she was never humiliated by the Garners, she could not feel her heart beating until she reached freedom in Ohio. And in consequence of the gradual collapse of Sweet Home, Paul D as well could sense the irony of the Garners' kindness: "Garner called and announced us men—but only on Sweet Home and by his leave" (220). By the time he finds Sethe long years after the attempted escape, he knows "It wasn't Sweet and sure wasn't home" (14). Sethe, too, realized that she could not love her children "proper in Kentucky because they wasn't mine to love . . . to get to a place where you could love anything you chose—not to need permission for desire—well now, *that* was freedom" (162). The Garners were kindhearted people but also participants in the system—nice Nazis, but Nazis nonetheless. By their accommodation of slavery, they made possible the prototypal evil of schoolteacher.

Schoolteacher symbolizes the most treacherous kind of institutional evil, the more threatening because it is not insane or barbaric or uncivil, the more frightening because it operates with the approval of a culture well able to guard its innocence under the guise of reason. Schoolteacher's ubiquitous notebook is emblematic of the disinterested scientific racism that has marked Western culture. His is a far more sinister evil than the atrocities perpetrated by his "nephews," for it attacks the very soul itself. Recalling schoolteacher's writing in his notebooks with ink she ironically prepared herself, Sethe tells Denver: "It was a book about us but we didn't know that right away. We just thought it was his manner to ask questions. . . . I still think it was them questions tore Sixo up. Tore him up for all time" (37). Later Sethe overhears schoolteacher instruct one of his pupils on how he should record Sethe's characteristics: "put her human characteristics on the left, her animal ones on the right" (193). A Dr. Mengele, schoolteacher projects a subtle evil wearing the mask of civilization. Only Sethe's unrestrained, irrational, barbarous act of love upon her child could stop him "in his tracks," a deed so morally reprehensible and monstrous that it seemingly exceeded even the horrific bestiality of the nephews that schoolteacher casually dismisses as unwise and counterproductive. While Morrison makes schoolteacher less a character than the embodiment of dehumanizing scientific rationalism, she reveals in Sethe the ineluctable duplicity of the human condition, the moral capacity both to choose and to bear the consequences of choice.

Sethe's first willful act, the escape from the Garner

estate, imitates the quest for freedom from a degenerate garden. Sweet Home echoes again the Romantic view of a flawed Eden, where the black slaves tolerated the loss of freedom because they lived in ignorance of their condition. After Mr. Garner's untimely death, they come to "know" the true conditions of their slavery, educated by schoolteacher and his nephews. In this initial fall they might be considered simply victims, like Adam and Eve in Romantic versions of the fall, unwitting prisoners of their own innocence. Once they move toward freedom north of the Ohio River (and east of their spurious Eden), they assume responsibility for their own "criminal" acts and become "victims" of their own flawed humanity as much as of the viciousness of whites. Indeed, their moral viability and superiority are measured by their ability to accept responsibility for their own involvement in Beloved's death. As the characters recount their past, made present in the resurrected Beloved, they must come to grips with the choices they have made, to acknowledge their lost innocence and attempt to recover wholeness. The moral judgments implicit in the individual stories allow no evasion of the truth as these characters wrestle with the presence of evil at large in the world and in themselves.

Of the main characters, Baby Suggs never recovers from such knowledge. She is another of the ancestor figures that surface in Morrison's fiction, like Eva Peace or Pilate or Thérèse, characters who, as noted earlier, "must defy the system . . . provide alternate wisdom, and establish and maintain and sustain generations in a land."[6] As an unchurched preacher she does not offer up the gospel of the organized church, but rather celebrates the freedom to be "in this here place, we flesh; flesh that weeps, laughs; flesh that dances on bare feet in grass. Love it. Love it hard. Yonder they do not love your flesh." Refer-

6. Toni Morrison, "City Limits, Village Values: Concepts of the Neighborhood in Black Fiction," in *Literature & the Urban Experience: Essays on the City and Literature*, ed. Michael C. Jaye and Ann Chalmers Watts (New Brunswick, N.J.: Rutgers University Press, 1981), 43.

ring to the destructive white culture "yonder," she tells the blacks gathered at the Clearing that "the only grace" they can have is "the grace they [can] imagine." Rejecting allegiance to a church too often hostage to the power that denied her all her children but Halle and crippled her body, she instructs the gathering to love the "flesh" that "here" abides in freedom, and "more than your life-holding wombs and your life-giving private parts, hear me now, love your heart. For this is the prize" (88–89). Yet even Baby Suggs, for all her "great heart" and insistence on self-love cannot counter the enormity of evil (and love) that destroys Beloved, and Baby Suggs has to accept this failure. She blames the whites: "The heart that pumped out love, the mouth that spoke the Word didn't count. They came in her yard anyway and she could not oppose or condemn Sethe's rough choice" (180).

But she also accuses herself. As Denver recognizes, Baby Suggs knows "the ghost [is] after Ma'am and her too for not doing anything to stop it" (209). She could not act then because the day schoolteacher and the others arrived she was already baffled by a "floating repulsion" she smelled in the air: "It wasn't whitefolks—that much she could tell—so it must be colored ones" (138). The "disapproving odor" is formed by her neighbors' anger at her elaborate feast the day before—"she had overstepped, given too much, offended them by excess" (138). Because she "over-stepped" ("Loaves and fishes were His powers—they did not belong to an exslave" [137]), she could not figure out the "dark and coming thing" she smelled "way back behind" the "floating repulsion." It was too late when she saw schoolteacher's high-topped shoes. Though she could not have prevented the slaughter, she judges herself guilty "for not doing anything about it." Devastated by the calamity, Baby Suggs thinks her "powerful Call" and message in the Clearing was "mocked and rebuked by the bloodspill in the backyard" (177). Though magnificent in her wisdom and tenacious in her love, Baby Suggs is "worn out" by a love so uncompromising as to warrant the slaughter of her grandchild. Her impotence in the presence of such appalling force convicts her of a fault, even though it was Sethe who acted. She goes to bed to die, "just grieving and thinking about colors and how she made a mistake" (209).

Stamp Paid and Paul D also share in a guilt that makes them morally alive, unlike the unconscionable whites who are the primary perpetrators of evil. Almost as soon as he shows Paul D the newspaper clipping about Sethe's murdering her child and explains it when it is clear his friend cannot read, Stamp feels a measure of remorse. He finds himself "not the high-minded Soldier of Christ he thought he was, but an ordinary, plain meddler" (170). When Paul D then leaves Sethe and goes to live in the cellar of the church, Stamp tries vainly to rectify his action. He pleads with Paul D: "She ain't crazy. She love those children. She was trying to outhurt the hurter" (234). Recognizing that he wants to judge Sethe just as the rest of the black community does, he futilely attempts "to get right with her and her kin" (181). Nor can the gentle Paul D claim innocence. Though he loves her, Paul betrays Sethe, fearful of the fierceness of her love. In the climactic moment when he judges Sethe for killing Beloved and "a forest [springs] up between them," he shifts his own guilt onto her. By now Beloved has already driven a wedge between Sethe and Paul and enticed him into spiritless sex in the cold-house where she has chased him from the house. So when he accuses Sethe of "too thick love" for her children and insists that there could have been "some other way," he shoves his own guilt onto Sethe's shoulders: "How fast he moved from his shame to hers. From his cold-house secret straight to her too-thick love" (165). Truly "blessed," Paul D nonetheless bears the mark of his fallen humanity when he deserts Sethe.

Although it is the community that eventually comes to cast out the demonic spirit at the end of the novel, the town blacks also prove culpable. Because of their condemnation of Sethe and Baby Suggs' feast, they refuse to warn them about the "new whitefolks with the Look. The Look every Negro learned to recognize along with his ma'am's tit. Like a flag hoisted, this righteousness tele-graphed and announced the faggot, the whip, the fist, the lie, long before it went public" (157). It is the moral indignation among the blacks that Baby Suggs had smelled the day of the disaster, and "It wasn't whitefolks." It was their "meanness" that allowed schoolteacher to find Sethe at the house. Like Baby Suggs, Stamp Paid, and Paul D, they share in a humanizing guilt denied the feckless whites with "the Look" of righteousness.

But of course it is Sethe who stands at the center of the moral ambiguity. Does Morrison ask us to see her as morally justified? Sethe tells Paul D that the murder achieved its end: "They ain't at Sweet Home. School-teacher ain't got em." He responds that "There could have been another way," but her retort "What way?" (165) remains unanswered. If Morrison does not resolve the question, it is not justified to accuse her of "lack of moral imagination" or a facile "determination to take no clear stand on the appalling actions she depicts."[7] Ambiguity, after all, is not a literary offense. The truth remains the paradox. Sethe could not have remained innocent whatever she chose. Either she would violate her love (she tells Paul D, "Love is or it ain't. Thin love ain't love at all." [164]) or offend the moral code. We might recall the 1977 interview in which Morrison commented that "with the best intentions in the world we can do enormous harm, enormous harm. . . . All about love . . . people do all sorts of things under its name, under its guise. The violence is a distortion of what, perhaps, we want to do."[8] *Beloved* takes this idea as far as it can go. To let Sethe off the hook entirely would reduce her as a character and, more significantly, simplify the moral complexity Morrison enjoins. Doubtless Sethe committed a criminal act of horrendous proportion. That she also commits a loving one in no way

7. Carol Iannone, "Toni Morrison's Career," *Commentary*, December 1987, 61.
8. Jane Bakerman, "The Seams Can't Show: An Interview with Toni Morrison," *Black American Literature Forum* 12 (1978): 160.

also information."[10] The knowledge it offers is the self-knowledge that comes only after the fall: "Me?" Sethe asks at the end—"Me?" (273).

* * *

In Toni Morrison's fiction characters one way or another enact the historical plight of blacks in American society. She offers no apology for her black female perspective. Though the black experience frames and informs her fictional narratives, it in no way reduces their universality. For all their complexity and diversity, the novels are woven together by common themes: the passage from innocence to experience, the quest for identity, the ambiguity of good and evil, the nature of the divided self, and especially, the concept of a fortunate fall. Morrison works the gray areas, avoiding simpleminded absolutes. Guitar tells Milkman at one point that "there are no innocent white people," but Milkman knows that there are no innocent blacks either, least of all himself. Blacks as frequently as whites inflict extreme physical and psychological violence on blacks: the Breedloves torment each other, and Cholly rapes his daughter; Eva Peace burns her son, and Nel and Sula betray the other self; Milkman callously rejects Hagar, and Guitar kills Pilate; Son takes revenge on the childlike Cheyenne, and Jadine abandons Son; Sethe murders her daughter, and Beloved demands uncompromising payment—and of course much more. There is no doubt, though, that underlying all these manifestations of cruelty is the pernicious racism of American culture which wields its power to pervert and distort the moral center. Clearly, Morrison wants us to see the most insidious form of evil in the malevolent ability of racism to misshape the human spirit.

Racism and oppression are not the exclusive properties

10. Bessie W. Jones, "An Interview with Toni Morrison," in Bessie W. Jones and Audrey L. Vinson, *The World of Toni Morrison* (Dubuque, Iowa: Kendall/Hunt, 1985), 136.

of white Americans, however, nor are blacks their only victims, as Morrison makes clear. Her moral vision allows for few single-minded villains or heroes. She asks us to distinguish between an Amy and a schoolteacher and to feel some compassion for white victims like Margaret Street. Furthermore, she creates black characters fully capable of moral choice. The whiteness she castigates represents the dehumanizing cultural values of a society given over to profit, possession, and dominance. It is a whiteness worn by blacks as well as whites. Most of Morrison's characters, black and white, earn a measure of condemnation and sympathy. She has said of them, "Some are good and some are bad, but most of them are both. I try to burrow as deeply as I can into a character. I don't come up with all good or all bad."[11]

Nor can Morrison's narratives be reduced to mere polemics. Employing what she refers to as a "black cosmology," Morrison does not reject so much as invert and amplify the Judeo-Christian tradition of Western thought, imitating something of the romantic interpretation of a fortunate fall. Her political vision proves especially suited to the theme. She transforms the orthodox garden in the conventional fall myth into settings that describe or caricature the white-constructed world where black characters are physically or psychologically bound and maimed: the Dick-and-Jane house in *The Bluest Eye*, the "Wright" home in *Sula*, Macon Dead's urban kingdom in *Song of Solomon*, L'Arbe de la Croix in *Tar Baby*, Sweet Home in *Beloved*. Each is a reflection of warped morality, of misplaced values that inhibit the assertion of self and racial consciousness of black characters. Morrison attacks those blacks who placidly adjust themselves to living in such specious gardens by playing it safe, "nesting," or living "in white face." The only hope for wholeness is a fall, a disruption of the enslaving powers and values that deny black authenticity. Blacks who rest secure in the conviction

11. Nellie McKay, "An Interview with Toni Morrison," *Contemporary Literature* 24, no. 4 (1983): 420.

of an externally defined righteousness become morally and existentially stunted; those who risk a fall bear the scars of their humanity. Conventional "goodness" leads to acquiescence, subservience, accommodation; "evil" paradoxically may lead to freedom, self-awareness, an authentic self. Like all fall myths, the novels depict, in Morrison's words, "a press towards knowledge," though often "at the expense of happiness."[12] The narratives interweave romantic rebellion and tragic possibility, mythic matter and intense realism, in the portrayal of lost innocence.

With the possible exception of Pecola, Morrison's protagonists undergo a process of becoming. When Pilate tells Ruth that there "ain't nothing going to kill [Milkman] but his ignorance" (140), she speaks metaphorically for the other black protagonists we have seen. They struggle to survive east of Eden in a chimerical world beyond good and evil. Here innocence cannot satisfy those who seek freedom from the subtle bondage of "mind forg'd manacles" that racism imposes under cover of moral certitude and judgment—chains formed of self-deprecation and feeble assent. Emancipation comes only by risking, and Morrison's characters achieve varying degrees of freedom in consequence of their falls: the unmitigated frenzy of Cholly's love locks Pecola Breedlove in childlike innocence; Nel Wright learns only in old age that she has given up her true self; Milkman Dead embraces his wholeness in ultimate confrontation with his Other; Jadine Childs evades her true self by returning to her white Eden; Sethe Suggs must pay the full cost for her criminality to earn her freedom. Save for Pecola, the main characters move toward the condition of tragedy: reliving the past in the present, suffering division and facing inevitable choice, choosing and bearing the consequences of choice—and all this action played out in a community given voice as a chorus and itself in need of resurrection.

Without significantly reducing the social commentary in her novels, Morrison's adaptation of the fall theme

12. Ibid., 424.

raises the works to a more universal level; without stereotyping characters as allegorical types, it gives them a symbolic dimension; without imposing structure, it provides an integrating pattern; and without sacrificing the novels' integrity, it allows for artistic ambiguity. Their duality exposed, the characters all seek equilibrium, struggling to exist in creative tension with their own dark sides. Cast from paradisiacal existence by virtue of their self-awareness, they all live after the fall. The "tar baby" that might yet ensnare them is vain but willful self-ignorance. They are convicted of their humanity in a world of competing values where "good" and "evil" constantly shift. In such a reality, a fall from innocence is essential to being, however frightening the risks, however ironic the end.

Morrison has commented, "I don't trust any judgment that I make that does not turn on a moral axis."[13] The moral perspective she offers permits no one the luxury of innocence. Ironically, Margaret Street speaks for Morrison's black heroes and heroines when she says, "Thank God I didn't get away scot-free" (235). As Milkman comes to understand, it is "the conviction of righteousness," more than any other force, that imprisons the self. Morrison has said of her fiction:

> But it is the combinations in characters that are the best part of writing novels—the combinations of virtue and flaw, of good intentions gone awry, of wickedness cleansed and people made whole again. If you judge them all by the best that they have done, they are wonderful. If you judge them by the worst that they have done, they are terrible.[14]

These are black characters convicted of their humanity, living after innocence in a world rife with tragic potential—with defeat and with victory.

13. Jones, "An Interview with Toni Morrison," 136–37.
14. McKay, "An Interview with Toni Morrison," 423.

INDEX

Wright's house as, 37, 42; in *Tar Baby*: Eloe as, 76; "Isle de Chevaliers" as, 63–80 *passim*, 96; mentioned, 53

God, 17, 19, 22, 23, 38, 73, 98

Good and Evil, Ambiguity of: in all novels, 95–98; in Cholly Breedlove's rape of Pecola, 10, 21, 81; in Eva Peace's burning of Plum, 31–32, 43, 81; in Sethe Suggs killing of Beloved, 21, 81

Grable, Betty: referred to in *The Bluest Eye*, 13, 19

Harlow, Jean: referred to in *The Bluest Eye*, 19

Harper, Frances, 6

Harris, Leslie, 46*n*2, 51

Harris, Trudier, 75*n*11

Hawthorne, Nathaniel: 5; Sethe Suggs compared to Hester Prynne, 91

Heinlein, Robert: *Stranger in a Strange Land* quoted, 44

House, Elizabeth, 79

Hurston, Zora Neale, 6

Iannone, Carol, 90

Imitation of Life: referred to in *The Bluest Eye*, 13, 19

James, Henry, 5

Jones, Bessie W., 63, 64, 66, 77–78

Kafka, Franz, 83

Kindermord: in *Beloved*, 21, 81–95 *passim*; in *Sula*, 31–32, 43, 81

Lee, Dorothy, 46*n*2, 58, 71

Lewis, R. W. B., 5–6

Lilith, 4, 36*n*15

Lydon, Susan, 78–79

Medea, 83

Melville, Herman, 70

Miller, Karl, 27*n*2, 33

Milton, John: *Paradise Lost*, 63*n*2

Miyoshi, Masao, 26–27

Morrison, Toni: and the Bible, 2–3; and the fortunate fall, 3–7 *passim*; on critics, 1–2; on ethnic literature, 1–2; on Western idea of beauty, 12; on political nature of literature, 82–83; view of evil in black community, 38

——Interviews: on "MacNeil-Lehrer Newshour," 83; with Jane Bakerman, 2, 21*n*7, 32*n*9, 36–37, 90; with Thomas LeClair, 3; with Nellie McKay, 2, 38, 65, 68, 96, 97, 98; with Gloria Nalor, 68*n*7; with Bettye J. Parker, 29, 31, 33, 40, 43; with Robert B. Stepto, 5, 12, 21, 22, 26, 31*n*7, 34, 42, 43*n*22; with Claudia Tate, 2, 21, 28–29, 37, 39

——Essays: "Behind the Making of *The Black Box*," 12; "City Limits, Village Values: Concepts of the Neighborhood in Black Fiction," 48, 87; "Memory, Creation, and Writing," 1, 2; "Rootedness: The Ancestor as Foundation," 1, 48*n*3, 53, 82

——Novels: *Beloved*: failure to win National Book Award, 1; Pulitzer Prize for Fiction, 1, 81; discussed, 81–95; mentioned, 4, 8, 21, 95, 96, 97; *The Bluest Eye*: discussed, 8–25; mentioned, 4, 6, 26, 30, 32, 33, 37, 45, 46, 95, 96, 97; *Song of Solomon*: debate about ending, 61–62; discussed, 45–62; mentioned, 1, 4, 5, 6, 8, 23, 28, 37, 68, 70, 77, 87, 95, 96, 97, 98; *Sula*: and Romantic literature, 26–28; discussed, 26–44; mentioned, 4, 5, 6, 8, 19, 23, 25, 45, 46, 47, 48, 50, 87, 95, 96, 97; *Tar Baby*: debate about ending, 77–

80; discussed, 63–80; mentioned, 4, 8, 23, 24, 54, 87, 95, 96, 97, 98

Nietzsche, Friedrich, 45

Oedipus, 83, 93
Ogunyemi, Chikwenye Okonjo, 16, 33n13, 36n14
O'Neill, Eugene, 5
Ostendorf, Berndt, 30
Other: related to idea of *Doppelgänger* or Divided Self in Romanticism, 26–28; in *The Bluest Eye*: Pecola Breedlove and Geraldine as Others, 15–16; Cholly and Pauline Breedlove as Others, 16–17; in *Song of Solomon*: Guitar Bains and Milkman Dead as Others, 50–62 *passim*; in *Sula*: Sula Peace and Nel Wright as Others, 26–44 *passim*; in *Tar Baby*: Son Green as Other, 65–80 *passim*. *See also* Serpent

Paleski, H. M., 27
Paradise. *See* Garden
Poe, Edgar Allan, 5

Rigney, Barbara Hill, 36n15
Rogers, Robert, 27n2
Romanticism: Morrison's affinity with, 26–29, 87

Royster, Phillip A., 36

Samuels, Wilfred D., 46n2
Schott, Webster, 69–70
Scruggs, Charles, 50, 53
Serpent: Cholly Breedlove as, 4; Guitar Bains as, 4, 47, 48–62 *passim*; Pilate Dead as, 46, 53; Sethe Suggs as, 4; Son Green as, 65–80 *passim*; Sula Peace as, 4, 28–44 *passim*. *See also* Other
Shelley, Percy Bysshe: *The Cenci*, 27
Smith, David, 93
Spiller, Robert, 5

Tate, Claudia, 2, 37
Temple, Shirley: referred to in *The Bluest Eye*, 8, 10, 12, 19, 23
Tragedy: Morrison's works as, 5; in *The Bluest Eye*, 10; in *Sula*, 39, 43–44; in *Tar Baby*, 78; in *Beloved*, 83, 85, 93, 94–95

Vinson, Audrey, 19
Violence, as distorted love: in *The Bluest Eye*, 21, 21n7; in *Beloved*, 90

Wagner, Linda, 24
Wegs, Joyce M., 61–62